Endorsements

The title of her book, *Priceless,* is who Billie Kaye is to me and multiple thousands of others. Whether she is speaking about worry, the battles that take place in our minds, the way we speak to others, or our understanding of the power of submission, Billie Kaye speaks biblical truth with great love. Her walk with the Lord and her love for her husband, Paul, are living examples of who she is. Thank you, Billie Kaye.

GEORGIA LEE PURYEAR

Billie teaches us in her beautiful book, *Priceless,* how to be a woman after God's own heart. To know Him. To love Him. To follow Him...and to enjoy the richest blessings He has for us when we do. Every woman's life will be more satisfying when her heart's desire is to do God's will. This resource is packed with practical advice and soul-inspiring insights that will increase your inner strength and peace. She teaches us the disciplines we can follow to lead a more passionate, devoted, and purposeful life. The power of a believing, praying wife, mother, and friend can never be underestimated. Thank you, Billie, for courageously sharing your story—one of love, faithfulness, mercy, and provision. You encourage and inspire us in your writing, teaching, and the example you graciously live every day. Billie, you are *priceless.* The journey is an exciting one. Thank you for helping us discover joy along the way as we seek to be the women God has called us to be. The woman you are.

JULIE DUNCAN

In this world where life can be hard, relationships strained, where we are undervalued, put down, and judged, always comparing our weaknesses to others' strengths, Billie Kaye brings a breath of life, empowering and refreshing our souls through truths from the Lord. Thank you, Billie Kaye, for reminding us that we are priceless. We all need to read this empowering book.

JOYA BAKER

Taking the reins in your life, holding on for dear life, being confident in the journey each day, and asking God to give you the wisdom and direction to follow His will in your life—I wish it was that easy! Thank you, Billie Kaye, for sharing your journeys, wisdom, and being so transparent to help the women in this world be the greatest gifts God designed us to be. We are blessed to have this *Priceless* book to learn from.

LESLIE WOLGAMOTT RICE

Billie Kaye is a woman of faith, strength, and lives her life by godly principles. The information she shares in her book will encourage and inspire you.

DARLENE A NELSEN

Billie Kaye truly exemplifies Psalm 119:11: *"Your word I have hidden in my heart, that I might not sin against You."* She knows the Word of God more than anyone I know, which is something I have admired about her since we've met. I am so excited she has chosen to take all of her knowledge and wisdom and share it with women in this book. Billie has written a must-read for women who want to deepen their faith and take control of their heart, their tongue, and their mind. Read this book and learn from one of the greatest examples of a woman in submission to God's Word.

MARCIE WHALEN

Priceless

Billie Kaye

A WOMAN OF STRENGTH

A WOMAN TO BE PRAISED

Billie Kaye Tsika

DESTINY IMAGE® PUBLISHERS, INC.

P.O. Box 310, Shippensburg, PA 17257-0310

"Promoting Inspired Lives."

This book and all other Destiny Image and Destiny Image Fiction books are available at Christian bookstores and distributors worldwide.

Cover design by Eileen Rockwell
Interior design by Terry Clifton
Author photo by Shelby Tsika, shelbytsikaphotography.com

For more information on foreign distributors, call 717-532-3040.
Or reach us on the Internet: www.destinyimage.com

ISBN 13 TP: 978-0-7684-5062-0
ISBN 13 EBook: 978-0-7684-5063-7
ISBN 13 HC: 978-0-7684-5065-1
ISBN 13 LP: 978-0-7684-5064-4

For Worldwide Distribution, Printed in the U.S.A.
1 2 3 4 5 6 / 22 21 20 19

Dedication

THIS BOOK IS DEDICATED TO ALL OF MY GIRLS, AND THE women God will add to this family. You are independent, strong, confident, and talented women of God. Perfect? No, but you are determined to live your lives to please the Lord and be godly women. You are on a journey in this life, so you will have much to learn. I'm still learning, too!

At times, you will make wrong decisions. But I am confident that you will learn from these decisions and be determined not to make the same mistakes again. You will face trials, heartache, loss, joy, sorrow, and setbacks. However, I know you will continue on your journey, not living in the regrets of the past, but looking to the future. I am a blessed woman to have such a tremendous group of women in my life.

My heart's desire for all of you is to love the Lord your God with all your heart, mind, soul, and strength. Fear the Lord, because this is the "beginning" of wisdom, and you will need wisdom to live in this world. You will need courage to stand for the truth. You will need confidence to face every situation God allows in your life. You will need a heart of forgiveness for the many offenses that will come your way. Let the "law" of kindness be on your tongue. Have a humble and giving heart. My love for you goes beyond words. Let your light shine!

Gretchen Ann Tsika Rush

Melanie Elaine Hadden Tsika

Kelley Lynne Stamey Tsika

Meagan Ashley Rush

Cathrine Emily Tsika

Marissa Alexandra Rush

Marlee Kaye Tsika

Shelby Nicole Tsika Marquardt

Malory Amelia Rush Northrup

Kadie Jewel Tsika

Kaleigh Elaine Kutac Tsika

Paxton Alyse Lutringer Tsika

Acknowledgments

I WANT TO SAY A SPECIAL THANK YOU TO MY DAUGHTER, Gretchen Ann Tsika Rush, for spending many hours proofing this book. She said, "You're like me, Mom, you write like you think, and that's not always good." In other words, there were lots of corrections. Everyone needs someone in their life to be completely honest with them. Thank you, my precious daughter, for not being afraid to confront when needed…but in a kind way.

As she read my manuscript she said, "Mom, you need to be honest about the first twenty years of your marriage. The ladies who read this may be going through a hard time and think you never had it bad, but have always had a great life. Yes, you have had a great marriage for these past thirty-something years, but you made a choice to 'stick with it' and now you are reaping the benefits." So, I say thank you to Gretchen for reminding me to write "the whole story."

Another special thank you to my hubby and best friend who has been the one to encourage me in every area of my life, and critique me, even when I didn't like it. He encouraged me to get serious about my singing, writing, and speaking. I am eternally grateful for God's greatest gift to me…Paul Edward Tsika Sr.

Thank you to my granddaughter Meagan Ashley Rush for helping me with the "Promises" by spending time on her computer while I was traveling.

Thank you to all of the women who sent their thoughts on the subject of "submission." I know it wasn't easy for some of you to be blatantly honest about your ideas and beliefs. However, I love how God has worked in all of our hearts to bring us to change through the truth of His Word.

Dr. J. Tod Zeiger: Tod has been a friend for many years. Paul and I have ministered together in Bible conferences with Tod. He has an excellent heart for the Lord along with a great gift for the family of God. His heart and giftedness continue to add tremendous value to Paul and me personally, as well as our ministry. He's an insightful man of God, and we are blessed to call him friend.

Destiny Image Publishers: Thank you. We have partnered with Destiny in publishing many of our books. They are a joy to work with and do an excellent job. A special thank you to Meelika Marzzarella and John Martin for their dedication to this project.

Contents

Foreword

WHEN I WAS ASKED TO WRITE THE FOREWORD FOR THIS book, I laughed. I asked, "Why me? Couldn't you find anyone better or more famous to write it?" She just laughed at me and didn't say anything. I thought about it for about five more seconds, maybe shorter, and then said, "Well, who better to write it than me?"

A Foreword is usually written by someone giving credibility to the author and the content of the book. Well, I have that covered. I not only know her very well, after all she is my mama, but I have watched her live what she has written in this book. I have seen the good, bad, and the ugly, or most of it, anyway.

The first time I read this book, I only had about half of it. I read it in about two hours. She asked me to go over it and make sure it was something that women would understand and be helpful to them; to make sure things made sense and that she wasn't being too preachy, or like she knew it all. I started reading it and couldn't put it down. Then she changed it on me, not a lot, but she did make it better! So, I had to start over!

I loved helping her edit the manuscript because I know she really means what she says. For fifty-one years I have

1

watched her live what she writes in this book, but most appreciated it for the past thirty-one years that I have been married. Growing up, I was always a daddy's girl, okay, okay, so I still am, and that won't ever change. However, I quickly became a mama's girl when I got married, and I've really grown into being more of one in the past three years.

Mark and I have lived most of our married life away from family, so three years ago when the opportunity came to live near my parents and do ministry with them, we did. I think this is what really made me appreciate my mama and the journey she has been on and the way she has led, and leads her life.

Growing up you see things through children and teenager eyes. I look back now, with somewhat more mature eyes, and see how God has used her to hold our family together.

Just the other day we were coming back from Houston and talking about the past. We were talking about how much she and my daddy went through when they were first married and how incredible it was that she stayed with him. You would have to hear their personal testimony to really understand. He wasn't a good man; and by all rights, she should have left. But I am so grateful and thankful that she didn't. And I don't even know most of how it was with them in the beginning, and I don't really want to know, but for her to stay was God and God alone. We both agreed. God had a plan—and *wow* did it work out for her and our family!

I told her that I want to be her when I grow up because I would never have stayed in that kind of marriage. I think deep, way deep down inside, she must have seen something in my daddy that made her want to see what could be or maybe it was just pure faith. Faith to believe that God could do anything—and He did!

Please understand that I am not in any way advocating for a woman to stay in an abusive relationship, and I really believe that is what theirs was, but because she stayed faithful and finally got a backbone—at least that is what I say—it worked out for them and our family.

Today, my daddy is an amazing, fearless, and wonderful husband, daddy, and pawpaw. I believe with my whole heart that it was God and my mama who made him into that man and, of course, his willingness to want to be that man of God for himself, Mama, and our family.

When I say she's got a backbone, that might not be the correct terminology, but it's the word I am using. She has always been headstrong, and since living near them these past three years, I really see it. When I tell people that she is more stubborn than daddy, they just look at me like I'm crazy or they don't believe me! She's just very quiet and subtle about it, mostly in a good way! She has a quiet strength that, when you really get to know her, you see it.

Everyone who meets her loves her, or they should! She has a strength about her that amazes me still to this day. She really has stayed the course in her life and marriage, and when she says what she says about attitude, submission, anxiety, the tongue, and so much more, she is saying it from experience and not just putting words on paper.

That doesn't mean she has done everything right or doesn't or hasn't made mistakes herself, but she is being very honest. I have seen her listen to my dad and do what he says with a good attitude and heart—and at other times, not so much. I have watched her "fight" back with him when she knew she was right and she wasn't going to be run over or bullied. I have seen her love with her whole heart and be the kind of wife I hope I am becoming.

She didn't just put words on paper to impress anyone or to make it seem like she is trying to be better than anyone. She is trying to help women become who God intended them to be and to be confident in who they are—to be wholly, truly, and totally content first in their relationship with the Lord because without Him we really can't do anything, and then be content in their relationship with their husband. Children, extended family, and all other relationships, come after these two. And my mama has lived that. She loves the Lord with her whole heart, soul, mind, and strength. And she has loved my daddy in the same way. This passage in the Bible is my mama:

> *Her children respect and bless her; her husband joins in with words of praise: "Many women have done wonderful things, but you've outclassed them all!" Charm can mislead and beauty soon fades. The woman to be admired and praised is the woman who lives in the Fear-of-God. Give her everything she deserves! Festoon her life with praises!* (Proverbs 31:28-31 The Message)

The English Standard Version of the Bible says it this way:

> *Her children rise up and call her blessed; her husband also, and he praises her: "Many women have done excellently, but you surpass them all." Charm is deceitful, and beauty is vain, but a woman who fears the Lord is to be praised. Give her of the fruit of her hands, and let her works praise her in the gates.*

I believe most women want this said about them, but they don't know how to get there. Read this book with an open heart and mind and you may just find yourself there. There will be times in the book when you will be angry, upset, and probably want to cuss a bit...I know I did. But when I went back over and reread it with my heart in the right place, I understood it better.

Two years ago, we celebrated my parents' fiftieth wedding anniversary! It was a great day with my brothers, their wives, my husband, and all of our children. There were twenty-two of us and we celebrated and laughed and cried. We have seen our parents in their bad times, not the worst, and thank You, Jesus, we didn't, and the good times, and I believe that we are a very blessed family. My parents aren't perfect, but they are parents who love each other with everything they are.

My mama wrote this book to help you, as a woman, to see where you can improve your marriage and family. It will help you:

- Have fifty-plus years together—and not just have the years, but to celebrate life with the husband God has for you, the husband you have chosen.

- Not be a pushover.

- Be okay to be you.

- Have a voice, to know that what you have to say is just as valuable as your husband's voice.

- Love, honor, and respect your husband and know when you don't agree, that is okay!

- Know that in those moments when everything seems to be falling apart and you can't go on and you can't get it together, your husband is not being who he should be, and your life seems to be in shambles…you can pray and give it all to God.

- Know God sees what is going on in your life and He has you in His hands.

- Know that it won't be easy but you can do it.

- Know that you are stronger than you think you are!

- Know you are going to make it!

I believe that when you read this book, you will be blessed by the words in it, the heart and wisdom behind it, and the application that is easy to see. Don't just read it, but *read* it. After each chapter, take time to pray, meditate on it, and then take what you need in that chapter and apply it to your life.

This book will be a book for your lifetime! A book that you can go back to countless times to reread and get something new out of it every time. It has taken my mama fifty-two years to write this book, a lifetime for some of us. And it is a book that I am so proud of. Proud to be the daughter who can write a Foreword for a mama who has lived, and lives, this book.

I love you, Mama, and way to go. This is an amazing book that I believe will help countless women when they read it!

—GRETCHEN RUSH
Proud Daughter of Billie Kaye Tsika

Introduction

WHEN I BEGAN TO PUT MY THOUGHTS ON PAPER, MY GOAL was simple, and my prayer straightforward: *Dear Lord, help me to communicate hope and encouragement to every woman who reads this book.* The last thing I want to have happen is for any woman to read my words and feel condemned, ashamed, or discouraged. If you have trusted Christ as Savior and Lord, you have every reason to live every day with His power to sustain you, no matter your circumstances.

Let's be honest—no one is immune from times of stress and uncertainty. Certainly, not me. When the enemy comes at me, instead of cowering in the corner, I come back by guarding my heart with the Word of God.

The following Scriptures, and more, remind me of two things:

1. The day I gave my life to Christ, He gave me abundant life now, and sure hope for the future. Jesus declares in John 10:10, *"The thief does not come except to steal, and to kill, and to destroy. I have come that they may have life, and that they may have it more abundantly."*

2. The apostle Paul's words remind me that because I am in Christ, there is no more condemnation.

Romans 8:1 says, *"There is therefore **now** no condemnation to those who are in Christ Jesus, who do **not** walk according to the flesh, but according to the Spirit."*

The following is an excerpt from *Father's Love Letter* by Barry Adams:

I don't care how many mistakes you've made. It doesn't matter how many bad choices you've made; nor does it make any difference how you were raised. I want you to know the depths of God's love for you. I want you to know how valuable you are. I want you to know that God created you for a purpose. He created you for greatness. You are not a mistake. All of your days are written in God's book. He's the One who determined when and where you would be born. You are fearfully and wonderfully made. He is your provider and will meet all of your needs. He is your greatest encourager. Nothing can separate you from His love. You are His treasured possession. He rejoices over you with singing. His plan for your future has always been filled with hope. If you seek Him with all of your heart, you will find Him. He has been misrepresented by those who don't know Him. It is His desire to lavish His love on you. He's your Father who comforts you in all of your troubles. God is for you not against you. Jesus' death on the cross was the ultimate expression of His love for you. In Christ, God's love for you is revealed. Nothing and no one can separate you from His love. How amazing is your Heavenly Father! His love for you exceeds anything you could ever ask or think. This is what I want you to know, but not just know, but truly believe.[1]

Wrapped up in God's marvelous grace is the fact you are not a mistake! God created you *on purpose, with a purpose,* before you even made an appearance on planet Earth. Greatness and purpose are encoded in your DNA, and there is nothing the devil can do about it.

Charles Swindoll made the following observation in his book *Grace Awakening:*

> This day—this very moment—millions are living their lives in shame, fear, and intimidation who should be free, productive individuals. The tragedy is they think it is the way they should be. They have never known the truth that could set them free. They are victimized, existing as if living on death row instead of enjoying the beauty and fresh air the abundant life Christ modeled and made it possible for all his followers to claim. Unfortunately, most don't have a clue to what they are missing. The whole package, in a word, is grace.[2]

When I started to write, some of my friends asked me, "What are you going to call your book?" I had to be honest and say, "I'm not sure exactly." I knew I wanted to cover *four issues* that affect most women. In my heart, I knew I had to write something about each one. Those four are: 1) worry and anxiety; 2) the battlefield of the mind; 3) the tongue; and 4) submission. Throughout this book we will be looking into each of these topics.

WORRY AND ANXIETY

There is a passage of Scripture that has been a mainstay in my life. I am referring to Philippians 4:6-8 (NIV):

Do not be anxious about anything, but in every situation, by prayer and petition, with thanksgiving, present your requests to God. And the peace of God, which transcends all understanding, will guard your hearts and your minds in Christ Jesus. Finally, brothers and sisters, whatever is true, whatever is noble, whatever is right, whatever is pure, whatever is lovely, whatever is admirable—if anything is excellent or praiseworthy—think about such things.

During times of worry and anxiety, I would always turn to this passage to keep my feet firmly planted on His promises.

THE BATTLEFIELD OF THE MIND

Revealed in the book is the fact that our most significant battles take place between our ears. Our mind is the battlefield; and if we don't employ our God-given weapons, we will stay hurt and wounded.

Our primary weapon against the attack of the enemy is the Word of God. Throughout, I use many Scriptures to get God's Word engrained in our hearts. Psalm 119:11 says, *"Your word I have hidden in my heart, that I might not sin against You."*

THE TONGUE

Probably the most influential member in our body—our tongue—is also discussed. The Book of James points out that this little member is so powerful that it has the ability to either cause trouble and heartache or joy and blessing. Words, good or evil, have consequences, so we must be careful how we use them.

SUBMISSION

This book covers an issue that has been a source of controversy among women for centuries—*submission*. This word is feared, misunderstood, and refused by so many. Just saying the word "submission" can cause some women to get on the defensive, or they look at me like I'm living in another century when I say we should be in submission to our husbands. I discovered a long time ago, if you want to start a heated discussion among women, bring up the word "submission" and stand back, the fireworks are about to go off!

I remember a few years ago talking with some women at a business meeting. In the context of our conversation, I referred to a Scripture passage using the phrase, "the Word of God." One of the ladies asked me, "What do you mean when you say the Word of God?" It hit me. I had been taking for granted that everyone would know what I meant when I used the phrase, "the Word of God." What was second nature to me did not translate to everyone I met. From that day forward, I tried to remind myself that some have never heard the Bible called the Word of God or know some of the words we Christians use on a daily basis.

No matter what phraseology you use, my desire is the same—to have God's Word be a major part of your life. I want every reader to love His Word and feast on the Bread of Life daily. I want you to thirst after the Word as a deer pants for water. I want readers' minds saturated with truth; after all, the Word of God is the only infallible, absolute truth in the universe.

As you read the following pages, you will discover that I use many personal illustrations to show women they are not alone in their struggles, especially when it comes to the four issues just listed. Many women have endured the heartache and devastation of trying to fill the emptiness of their hearts by turning to alcohol, sex, or drugs. And, in most cases, it doesn't take very long to discover that adding more substitutes for the love of God only makes matters worse, not better.

We all have our battles through life, especially in a marriage. This joining of lives, male and female, can be the biggest joy and reward—or it can be the most devastating and heartbreaking. It all comes down to choices!

The greatest joy in my life was the day I understood that God put me here for a purpose. We are wanderers on this earth for as many years as the Lord has ordained, and we all have a purpose. It is up to us to discover what that purpose is. I believe with all my heart that God is my Father and loves me unconditionally, so I want my life to count for Him.

So, let me ask you a question. Why are you here on this earth? What is your purpose?

I have four desires that I believe are my purpose.

My first and greatest desire is to love the Lord with all of my heart and with all my soul and with all my strength and with all my mind. Jesus said this is the first and greatest commandment, and the second is to love my neighbor as I love myself (see Matthew 22:37-39).

Second, I want to be the greatest helpmeet that I can be for Paul, my husband. I want to help him fulfill the purpose God has for him; in doing that, I fulfill my purpose.

My third purpose was to raise godly children, which I did. I'm not saying they have always been this way, or that they didn't have their struggles in their younger years, but they are a joy to my heart today. They have fulfilled my desire.

The fourth purpose is to be content right where I am and with who I am. I don't want anyone else's life. I don't want what anyone else has. I don't want to be like anyone else. I don't want to look like anyone else. I just want to be me, because that's who God made me to be.

> *The purposes of a person's heart are deep waters, but one who has insight draws them out* (Proverbs 20:5 NIV).

My prayer is that you will be encouraged, blessed, healed, restored, and renewed as you read this book. Maybe not so much by the words I write, but more so by the *truth* from God's Word that I share with you. As you prepare your heart to read the following pages, let me share something that I read several years ago that spoke to my heart. I thought I would share it with you to let you know how precious you are to your heavenly Father. We are all being *kept!*

> You see, there were a few times when I thought I would lose my mind, but God kept me sane (Isaiah 26:3).
>
> There were times when I thought I could go no longer, but the Lord kept me moving (Genesis 28:15).
>
> At times, I've wanted to lash out at those whom I felt had done me wrong, but the Holy Ghost kept my mouth shut (Psalm 13).
>
> Sometimes, when I thought the money wasn't going to be enough, God kept the lights on, the water on, the car paid, the house paid, etc. (Matthew 6:25-34).
>
> When I thought I would fall, He kept me up. When I thought I was weak, He kept me strong! (1 Peter 5:7; Matthew 11:28-30).
>
> I could go on and on and on, but I'm sure you hear me! Praise the Lord and pass the filet mignon! I'm blessed to be "kept."
>
> Are you...or do you know a "kept" woman? If so let her know she is "kept!"[3]

ENDNOTES

1. Barry Adams, "Father's Love Letter," Crossway; https:// www .crossway.org/tracts/fathers-love-letter-3049/; accessed December 19, 2018.

2. Charles R. Swindoll, *The Grace Awakening* (Dallas, TX: Word Publishing, 1990), 4.

3. Author Unknown, "I'm a Kept Woman"; Refreshing Times for Women (blog); https://thetimesofrefreshing.wordpress .com/words-of-encouragement/im-a-kept-woman/; accessed May 9, 2018.

Chapter 1

You Really Can Trust God

Know therefore that the Lord your God is God,
he is the faithful God, keeping his covenant
of love to a thousand generations of those who
love him and keep his commandments.
—Deuteronomy 7:9 NIV

WHEN I STARTED WRITING THIS BOOK FOR WOMEN, I HAD typed about eighteen pages when I decided to take a break. I continued my reading from a devotional book by Ken Gire titled *Windows of the Soul.*

As I was reading one of the chapters, my heart was broken after reading about a couple who had wonderful dreams and plans for their future. However, after just a couple of years of marriage, illness led to loss of jobs. They now had to consider what the future held for them. They faced the constant care for both of them because of their debilitating health conditions. There was no income to pay someone to care for them, and they would never have the children they so desperately wanted.

Now this couple was facing the realization that their dreams of serving the Lord in another country would never come to fruition. In all of this, they never got angry at God. They never got bitter. They didn't curse God! They knew He was their only hope. They knew they had to embrace the promises of God and trust their heavenly Father—knowing that He had them in His embrace and would take care of them. Oh, I'm sure they had days of doubt. After all, great believers are great doubters! We all fall into that category at times.

I continued to weep as I turned to read the next chapter about a young woman who had been abused in her childhood. She didn't realize how much hurt she was carrying until God began a deep work of healing in her.

As I read these two stories, I knew I had never suffered in this way. I never had to face what so many men and women faced, or are facing in their lives. I had never been abused as a child or had a parent abandon me. I didn't know what it felt like to have been bedridden with no hope of recovery. I've never lived in a war-torn country where I feared for my children's lives on a daily basis. There were so many things I thought of as I went back in my mind about what I had written on those first few pages.

I thought to myself, *Who am I to be advising women? I haven't been through the kind of trauma some of these women have been through, nor do I understand what hurt is! I don't understand the mental cruelty some have had to endure. I don't understand the heartache of losing a child. I had two wonderful parents who loved me and raised me the best they knew how. I have a wonderful husband who loves me. I have three children who are married and doing fantastic, ten wonderful grandchildren who are the delight of my life, and two precious great-grandsons whom I love with all of my heart. My life is blessed! My life is awesome! My life is a life with so much joy and peace and abundance!*

Yes, these thoughts bombarded my mind and put me under condemnation. I know, there's no condemnation (see Romans 8:1) to those who are in Christ Jesus, but I'm just being honest about what my thoughts were at this time after reading about the heartache of only three people. But then the Holy Spirit reminded me that I had suffered much, but maybe not in the way others had.

For five years, before my husband Paul came to Christ, he was verbally, emotionally, and a few times even physically abusive. Also, after he came to Christ, he battled for years with some of the same tendencies. I suffered for many years, silently, as he worked through his own issues. But that didn't lessen the verbal and emotional abuse I felt in our relationship.

In the end, suffering is suffering, and it doesn't really matter how it comes about, whether it was self inflicted or brought on by someone else or whether it was wrong choices on your part or on the part of others. So, I realize I can be counted among those women who have had their own difficult journey to work through. But during these times and more was when God not only protected me but taught me the most valuable lessons of relational life in marriage.

When Paul came out to where I was sitting, I broke down weeping and shared what I was feeling. He understood because he has experienced the same thoughts and feelings. We know without a doubt that every good and perfect gift comes from the Lord, and we don't ever want to despise all that God has given us and all He's done for us. He's the One in control. He's the One who gives gifts—every good and perfect gift comes from our Father (see James 1:17). We wrestle with these feelings of unworthiness even though our hearts are so full of thanksgiving and praise for the life God has allowed us to live on this earth.

ANOTHER PERSON'S BLESSING

I thought of a message Paul has preached many times out of Matthew 20. The parable is about a man who owned a vineyard. He hired men to work at different hours of the day and promised all of them a day's wage. When the day had ended and the men came to get their pay, everyone got the same amount. The men who had worked eight hours received the same as the ones who worked just one hour.

As you might expect, the men who worked longer hours began to complain, "Hey, we worked a lot longer than these others. Why are they getting the same amount as us?" The owner said to the men, "I didn't take from you to give to them. I promised you a day's wage, and that's what you got. I also promised a day's wage to those who worked only one hour. I have paid what I promised."

The points Paul gave while preaching this message have never left me:

1. You always get better pay when you let God keep the books.

2. It's always too early to quit, but it's never too late to start.

3. God's not fair, but He is just!

4. Another person's blessing is never your loss.

That last point is the one I remind myself of often—*another person's blessing is never my loss.* I absolutely understand and believe that to be true! So, why do I allow the enemy to discourage me? Why do I feel unqualified to receive God's blessings? Why do these thoughts of unworthiness creep into my mind?

As I thought about this message, my questions were many about the ones who had worked just one hour:

- How did they respond when they received the same pay as the workers who worked ten hours or eight hours?

- Were they grateful or did they feel guilty and feel unworthy because they didn't work as long and yet received the same pay as those who bore the heat of the day? ·

- Or, did they walk away saying, "Na-na-na-na-na," like we used to do when we were children and wanted to let others know we had won?

The story doesn't tell us, so we are left to our own conclusions.

I don't know about you, but I know in my heart I want to be humbled and thankful for receiving such abundant pay for so little work. I don't want to feel unqualified, unworthy, or allow the enemy to discourage me from God's blessings.

God doesn't take from someone else to give to me, and He doesn't take from me to give to someone else. He has enough in His storehouse to meet every need of every one of His children. He's the Keeper of the vineyard! I don't have to feel guilty or condemned for all the blessings from God. I can rejoice and be glad for others and myself. After all, it's His prerogative to do with His gifts precisely what He wants. The vineyard keeper's question to the complainers was, "Do you begrudge My generosity?" My answer to His question is "NO! I don't begrudge anything You do! I know You are a just God. I will trust You with all my heart."

TRUST GOD AND FORGIVE

I know what I've written in the following pages is true, and I know we can trust God in every situation because His Word is faithful and He's true to His promise to take care of us. I want you to know that I am not writing this book with a flippant attitude and saying, "Just get over it and make right choices." I know it's not easy, at times, to work through some of the pain and heartache that has been part of so many lives.

I know there are times we have to say, "I forgive" over and over to remind ourselves that we have chosen to forgive someone. We also have to remember that it's God who forgives us. First John 1:9 tells us, *"If we confess our sins, He is faithful and just to forgive us our sins and to cleanse us from all unrighteousness."*

Self will continually condemn, so we have to remind ourselves that God has forgiven us, and we can be assured that He is faithful. There are times we have to tell ourselves that we are trusting God for our every need. There are times we have to encourage ourselves in the Lord and believe that we are healed in Jesus' name, we are renewed in Jesus' name, and we are overcomers in Jesus' name.

REMEMBER

Deuteronomy is the book of remembrance. Moses wrote it to the new generation destined to possess the Promised Land that was promised to their parents when they were delivered from Egypt. Moses wanted them to remember how God saved their parents from slavery. He also wanted them to remember that their parents rebelled and ended up spending forty years in the desert because of their unbelief. They were not allowed to enter the Promised Land.

Yes, God supplied their needs while wandering in the desert, but only Joshua and Caleb, the two spies who believed

God, and those who were twenty-five years and younger, entered the Promised Land. Their parents forfeited the promised blessings of God because of unbelief, disobedience, and ungratefulness.

The last message from Moses in Deuteronomy was *remember, remember, remember.* He recounted the whole story to this new generation to remind them of God's faithfulness. He wanted to encourage the Israelites to believe and obey God so they could receive His blessings. We are no different from the Israelites. I believe we have to be continually reminded of God's promises and remember all He has done and is doing for us.

Bible teacher Jenny Salt shared an illustration that reminded me that when it comes to God's faithfulness, we need to ask Him to show us a wider frame, not just a single snapshot. Or, as Jenny Salt observed, "We must have the bigger picture."

She stated:

> A few years ago, there was an ad on TV that started like this: There was a woman sitting in a car. She minds her own business, and suddenly this man comes out of the blue, rips the door open, grabs her, and pulls her out of the car roughly. It looks like he's attacking her, and we look on in horror. Then the camera pulls back, and we see that the car is actually on fire, but the woman didn't know it. The man wasn't assaulting the woman, he was rescuing her. The ad finishes by saying, "You need the bigger picture. Channel 10 News gives you the bigger picture."
>
> The ad makes a good point. We need to have the bigger picture. And in the Book of Joshua, the people of Israel needed to have the bigger picture. As they

21

looked in the direction of the Jordan River, knowing they'd have to cross it and then face cities and people who were big and powerful, the people of Israel were overwhelmed and afraid. The bigger picture, though, is that the Lord God had promised the Israelites that they would enter the land. They were not alone nor forsaken. God would do all that he said he would do. That's the bigger picture. God was faithful and in control. You need the bigger picture.[1]

We must remember on those days when we don't have all the answers, or the bigger picture, that God has our best interests at heart. Trusting in His plan for our lives is crucial. Especially during those times when we get confused and discouraged when things don't go the way we think they should.

As the old hymn declares:

Trust and obey,
For there's no other way
To be happy in Jesus,
But to trust and obey.[2]

My prayer is that you will be encouraged, blessed, healed, restored, and renewed as you read this book. Maybe not so much by the words I write, but more so by the *truth* from God's Word that is contained in this writing.

ENDNOTES

1. Jenny Salt, "The Big Picture of God's Faithfulness," Christianity Today International; https://www .preachingtoday.com/sermons/sermons/2011/october/ godsfaithfulness.html; accessed May 25, 2018.

2.   The refrain from "Trust and Obey" by John Henry Sammis (1846-1919); https://www.hymnal.net/en/hymn/h/582; accessed May 27, 2018.

Chapter 2

Only Jesus Meets Your Deepest Needs

Come, all you who are thirsty, come to the waters; and you who have no money, come, buy and eat! Come, buy wine and milk without money and without cost. Why spend money on what is not bread, and your labor on what does not satisfy? Listen, listen to me, and eat what is good, and you will delight in the richest of fare.
—ISAIAH 55:1-2 NIV

I HAVE HEARD MANY WOMEN TALK ABOUT HOW DISCONtented they are because their husbands aren't meeting their needs. A simple definition of "discontentment" is a restless desire or craving for something one does not have.[1] They want their husbands to make them happy, keep them satisfied and content, and most of all, they want their husbands to meet *every* need in their lives. Well, let me assure you that when you look to another human being to meet your *every* need, male or female, you will stay dissatisfied and discontented.

There's only one true Source for all of our fulfillment and the answer to the longings of our heart—Jesus. There's an old song by Lanny Wolfe titled, "Only Jesus Can Satisfy Your Soul." One line in the song says it all: "Only Jesus can satisfy your soul. Only He can change your heart and make you whole. He'll give you peace you never knew, sweet love and joy and heaven too, only Jesus can satisfy your soul."[2]

In 1974, in the nursery at Lazbuddie Baptist Church, I trusted Christ as my Lord and Savior. I know that I know that I know that Jesus changed my life that night. However, for many years after, I relied on, depended on, and trusted in Paul to meet all of my needs and the desires of my heart. I didn't realize I was doing this until God intruded into my life in the mid-1980s in a way I would never have expected. I will share more about His intrusion later.

In truth, my husband Paul became an idol. Anything you desire more than God or put in place of God, whether it's dreams, gifts, spouse, children, business, or callings, even though they may be God-ordained, He may take them away until you get your desires right. He usually gives them back when they cease to become idols and you can see them in the right light.

In John chapter 4, there's a story about a Samaritan woman that illustrates my point. A woman from Samaria came to draw water, and John 4:7-10 gives us the heart of the conversation:

Jesus said to her, "Give Me a drink." For His disciples had gone away into the city to buy food. Then the woman of Samaria said to Him, "How is it that You, being a Jew, ask a drink from me, a Samaritan woman?" For Jews have no dealings with Samaritans. Jesus answered and said to her, "If you knew the gift of God, and who it is

who says to you, 'Give Me a drink,' you would have asked
Him, and He would have given you living water."

This woman thought Jesus was talking about drawing water from the physical well. There are times when, like this woman, we seek water from a physical well rather than the Living Well—Jesus. She thought another husband would fill that thirst in her life; after all, Jesus said she had been married five times and the one she was living with at the time wasn't her husband. Jesus answered her, *"Everyone who drinks this water will get thirsty again and again. Anyone who drinks the water I give will never thirst—not ever. The water I give will be an artesian spring within, gushing fountains of endless life"* (John 4:13-14 The Message). When Jesus said that anyone who drinks the water He gives will *"never thirst—not ever,"* that's a double negative in the Greek language. He was telling the Samaritan woman and saying to us that we *will never, no not ever* thirst again. That may be bad grammar, but it's great theology. That's His promise as we drink from the well that *never* runs dry—Jesus.

I was like this Samaritan woman. I trusted in Paul—the physical water well—rather than the Living Well, Christ. I wanted Paul to meet all of my needs. I trusted him to fulfill the longings of my heart. I didn't look at him as God, he thinks I did, but I was putting him in the place where only God belongs. I set Paul up on a pedestal, so God proceeded to knock him off. I believe God will knock off all of the gods we have put on a pedestal.

I couldn't blame Paul for my choice. He didn't put himself up on that pedestal. I'm the one who trusted in a human being to meet my *every* need. I knew what the first commandant was, but I was blinded. God removed the blinders! He alone is on that throne now. I did get a sign for our bathroom that says, "My husband and I have different religions.

He thinks he's God and I don't." Just a joke. We tend to be like this Samaritan woman who was drawing water from a well that would eventually run dry, rather than drinking from the Living Well who would quench her thirst. To experience true fulfillment, we must continually drink from the Living Well.

Are you thirsty? Do you believe that another house will quench that thirst? Another car? Another child? More money? Bigger business? A career? A husband, or a different husband? I can assure you, my dear friend, that nothing and no one will ever quench that thirst except Jesus. He can and will fill that longing in your soul, all you have to do is ask.

If we aren't careful, we will put our trust in things or people. And before we know it, we wake up one day and realize something or someone has replaced God on the throne of our heart. Yes, they have become our idols.

Deuteronomy 5:7 is very clear as to God's attitude when it comes to idols, *"You shall have no other gods before Me."* Bible teacher Robert Driskell wrote an online article titled, "You Shall Have No Other Gods Before Me: Lesson and Life Application." In sharing his thoughts, he made the following observation:

> The first of the Ten Commandments God gave to Moses reads thus from the English Standard Version of the Bible: "You shall have no other gods before me" (Exodus 20:3). It would seem that anyone who understands just Who God is, would have no trouble putting Him first in their lives. Believers should almost automatically center their lives around worshiping Him. However, the biblical record, and the practical experience of believers everywhere, reveals that professing believers too often consider faithfulness to God a secondary, or minor, priority. I have

written, in my book *Spiritual Suicide: The Crisis of Casual Christianity,* that one of the biggest problems with Christianity today is that Christians do not take seriously enough their relationship with God. Many professing believers consider God to be merely an add-on to their lives instead of our Source, Reason, Judge, Sustainer, Savior, and Future.

The phrase, "No other gods before me" does not mean that God merely wants us to organize our gods with Him at the top. It does not mean that, as long as we worship God first, we are free to have other gods also. It means that there are to be no other gods in our lives but the one true God. The word translated "before" in this verse does not have to do with time or ranking. It is saying that we are to have no other gods in God's sight. In other words, we are to worship nothing else in our lives but the one true God. He is worthy of our complete and total commitment.[3]

We can't work hard enough to quench that thirst. But our God promises to supply all of our need according to His riches in glory by Christ Jesus (see Philippians 4:19). Some people believe that money can buy anything and everything they need. But, my dear friend, real peace with God cannot be purchased, only received as a free gift. There is peace while we live and peace when we die. Nor can we buy health or agape love. We can't buy true joy. It doesn't matter how wealthy a person is, these things come only from the Lord. The truly important things in life are not purchased with money.

In John 6:32-35, Jesus told His disciples and the people gathered to hear Him that He is the bread of life, and if they come to Him they will never hunger, and if they believe in Him they will never thirst.

Centuries before Jesus was here on the earth, the prophet Isaiah declared:

> *The poor and needy seek water, but there is none, their tongues fail for thirst. I, the Lord, will hear them; I, the God of Israel, will not forsake them. I will open rivers in desolate heights, and fountains in the midst of the valleys; I will make the wilderness a pool of water, and the dry land springs of water.*

What a great promise from Isaiah 41:17-18. Yes, He's speaking to the ones He delivered from Egypt, but this promise is for His children today as well—for you and for me. We are all poor and needy. But when we are poor and needy, our God is merciful and gracious. And the more poor and needy we see ourselves, the more merciful and gracious He will be toward us. The Lord will not forsake us or ever leave us alone. He won't just give us a drink, He will make the desert a mighty river! He will flood us with His love. He will flood us with His joy. He will flood us with His peace. Hallelujah!

The following is an old song that reminds us to keep our eyes on the right Person, Christ alone:

> *O soul, are you weary and troubled?*
> *No light in the darkness you see?*
> *There's a light for a look at the Savior,*
> *And life more abundant and free!*
> *Turn your eyes upon Jesus,*
> *Look full in His wonderful face,*
> *And the things of earth will grow strangely dim,*
> *In the light of His glory and grace.*[4]

Hebrews 12:1-2 says:

Therefore we also, since we are surrounded by so great a cloud of witnesses, let us lay aside every weight, and the sin which so easily ensnares us, and let us run with endurance the race that is set before us, looking unto Jesus, the author and finisher of our faith, who for the joy that was set before Him endured the cross, despising the shame, and has sat down at the right hand of the throne of God.

Are you tired of being weary? Are you tired of being troubled, angry, anxious, afraid, and frustrated? Let's look to God's Word for the solution.

All Scripture is God-breathed and is useful for teaching, rebuking, correcting and training in righteousness, so that the servant of God may be thoroughly equipped for every good work (2 Timothy 3:16-17 NIV).

Let me encourage you to read every Scripture that is cited in this book. You may not remember what I write, but God's Word will not return to Him void. The truth of God's Word will accomplish what God wants to accomplish in your life.

*Just as rain and snow descend from the skies and don't go back until they've watered the earth, doing their work of making things grow and blossom, producing seed for farmers and food for the hungry, so will **the words that come out of my mouth** not come back empty-handed. **They'll do the work I sent them to do, they'll complete the assignment I gave them** (Isaiah 55:10-11 The Message).*

ENDNOTES

1. Definition of discontent; http://www.dictionary.com/browse/discontentment; accessed June 15, 2018.

2. Lanny Wolfe, "Only Jesus Can Satisfy Your Soul," http://barryshymns.blogspot.com/2010/05/only-jesus-can-satisfy-your-soul.html; accessed June 18, 2018.

3. Robert Driskell, "You Shall Have No Other Gods Before Me: Lesson and Life Application," What Christians Want to Know; https://www.whatchristianswanttoknow.com/you-shall-have-no-other-gods-before-me-lesson-and-life-application/#ixzz5J4Zb0PfT; accessed June 18, 2018.

4. Helen H. Lemmel (1863-1961), *Baptist Hymnal: Turn Your Eyes upon Jesus* (Nashville, TN: Convention Press, 1975), 198.

Part I

Experiencing the Peace of God?

Anxiety: apprehensive uneasiness or nervousness usually over an impending or anticipated ill: a state of being anxious; a strong desire sometimes mixed with doubt, fear, or uneasiness.[1]

Chapter 3

Why Worry When You Can Rest?

*Do not be anxious about anything, but in everything
by prayer and supplication with thanksgiving let your
requests be made known to God. And the peace of God,
which surpasses all understanding, will guard your
hearts and your minds in Christ Jesus. Finally, brothers,
whatever is true, whatever is honorable, whatever is
just, whatever is pure, whatever is lovely, whatever
is commendable, if there is any excellence, if there is
anything worthy of praise, think about these things.*
—Philippians 4:6-8 ESV

PHILIPPIANS 4:6-8 HAS BEEN A MAINSTAY IN MY LIFE FOR
many years. I have many favorite verses, but the apostle Paul's
words of encouragement to the folks in Philippi have seen me
through many fierce battles. I would encourage you to memorize these verses, as we all will need them to get us through
some rough days.

When I looked up the word "anxious," I found more than fifty words that describe a person who is anxious. However, I think the following seven words that I've listed will give you an idea of what anxiety embodies. Some definitions for anxiety are: *afraid, apprehensive, careful, concerned, disquieted, fretful, worried.*

ANXIETY

Before I share with you my understanding of what the Bible teaches about anxiety, I recognize there are physical and biological reasons for anxiety and depression. We have experienced this in our own family, so please don't get defensive when you read this section of my book. I'm not condemning anyone or saying your disease is caused by you not trusting God. I know we all suffer from different kinds of physical and biological maladies.

However, there are those who are anxious and worried because they are not trusting God; otherwise, Paul's words would have been meaningless if it were not the case. Why tell people not to worry or be anxious if they were not having the issue? It can be a choice we make even as Christians.

I believe the first time I began to understand about not being anxious was when Paul and I drove our daughter, Gretchen, to Lynchburg, Virginia, to attend Liberty University in 1985. After all, she was our firstborn and only daughter, and I knew she was a little rebellious, so I was very apprehensive about leaving her so far away from us. At the time, we lived in Zachary, Louisiana, which is a long way from Lynchburg. So, you can understand my feelings of anxiety.

After Gretchen was settled in, Paul and I got in the car and started our long drive back to Louisiana. Let me tell you, it was a sad but happy time! Oh, I knew she was in God's hands, but it was hard letting go. I really don't remember being anxious or worried about leaving her there, but I was worried and anxious about her being content and happy. I wanted her to enjoy her college years and be grateful for this opportunity. I wanted her to look to the future with great hope and expectation. Most of all, Paul and I were trusting God to help her find a godly man who would love her and lead her in the right direction, which He did.

What good would it have done for me to worry? Could I have changed her heart? Could I control what she was doing? No! The only thing I could do was pray for her and trust her into God's loving hands. Someone might say, "Taking a child to college is not a situation to get anxious or worried over. There are more serious matters." That's true, but for me, at that time in my life, it was serious. I believe it was a test from the Lord. He wanted me to trust Him with this precious gift He had blessed Paul and me with for eighteen years.

We can't judge what someone else is going through or know where they are in their Christian journey. We don't know what they had to endure or how mature they are in their faith. And, we don't know what God is trying to teach them. One thing I have learned is we never know what tests are ahead for any of us. God prepares us for everything He takes us through, whether it's leaving a child at the university, seeing them off as they join the military, crying happy tears at their wedding, or seeing them sick in a hospital bed. I've heard it said, "God tests us to strengthen and grow us; Satan tempts us to discourage and destroy us."

"YOU—FOLLOW ME"

There's a portion of Scripture in the Book of John, in chapter 21, where Jesus was talking to the disciples after the resurrection. He asked Peter three times if He loved him. Peter answered yes, all three times. And three times Jesus told Peter to "Feed My sheep." Then He proceeded to tell Peter how he would die. I'm sure Peter was thinking, *Well, if this is the way I will die, how about John?* So Peter asked Jesus what was going to happen to John. I love the way John 21:22-23 reads in The Message Bible, *"Jesus said, 'If I want him to live until I come again, what's that to you? You—follow me.'"* I remember a woman coming up to Paul in a revival meeting talking about another church member whom she felt "got away" with something and wanted her "straightened out." He quoted this verse to her and then simply said, in a kind way, "That's none of your business, what is that to you. You just keep your eyes on Jesus and let Him tend to that person." I believe we all need to remember this, don't you?

This lady was only seeing and judging from her perspective.

We see the outward, and God sees the heart. We are so quick to judge others, yet get upset when someone judges us because we know they don't know our whole story. We want them to have compassion and understanding toward us, yet we forget it goes both ways. What is the Golden Rule? God's Word tells us in Luke 6:31 that we should treat others the way we want to be treated. In other words, do unto others as you would have them do to you, not as they do to you! If we want compassion, we need to show compassion. If we want forgiveness, we must give forgiveness. If we set ourselves up as the judge, we will be judged the same way.

What I discovered when I searched the web for anxiety quotes were some good quotes, and yet other quotes that seem to point to an epidemic of sadness and anxiety in this world. So many quotes were from people who have lost hope, who are afraid of the future, who have regrets from their past, who have been abandoned by fathers, mothers, and spouses, and those who feel like they will never measure up. No matter how anxious we are, we can't change the future, and no amount of regret can change the past. Most of the things we are anxious or worried about don't happen.

Psalm 118 says it's better to trust God than people. Absolutely. It reminds us that God is our strength and song. He is our salvation. He is our refuge. He's our shelter in a storm. Then the psalmist declares that, *"This is the day the Lord has made; we will rejoice and be glad in it"* (Psalm 118:24). He made a choice to rejoice and be glad. This is what we must do to combat anxiety. But how? Just before the apostle Paul said, *"Don't be anxious,"* he said, *"Rejoice in the Lord always. Again I will say, rejoice!"* (Philippians 4:4). I don't believe we can be worried and anxious when we're rejoicing in the Lord.

John Edmund Haggai wrote a wonderful book titled *How to Win Over Worry*. In discussing this very issue, he wrote:

> Count your blessings. If it will help you, take time every now and then to write out your blessings on a piece of paper. Praise God for the love of your wife, the affection of your children, your good health, the encouragement of your friends. As you exert some effort along this line, blessings by the score will come crowding into your consciousness. You will soon feel your heart singing, "Praise God from whom all blessings flow!" And you will be honoring the Lord as you obey the exhortation in Philippians 4:4 that we are to rejoice always.[2]

In his online devotional, "The Unspoken Source of Anxiety," Max Lucado asks the question, "How can a person deal with anxiety?" His answer is priceless: You might try what one fellow did. He worried so much that he decided to hire someone to do his worrying for him. He found a man who agreed to be his hired worrier for a salary of $200,000 per year. After the man accepted the job, his first question to his boss was, "Where are you going to get $200,000 per year?" To which the man responded, "That's your worry."[3]

How can we win the war over worry? Our minds must be renewed—and the only way to renew our minds is by the washing of the water of the Word. God's Word is like a bar of soap. When our hands are dirty, we must use soap to clean them. When our minds need cleansing, renewing, it must be by the Word of God. There's no shortcut. God has empowered us to be able to think in a godly manner.

Titus 3:3-7 says God's kindness and love appeared to us, not by anything we did or didn't do, but by His mercy He saved us. How? By birthing us into His kingdom we were born again by the renewing of the Holy Spirit. God sent His Holy Spirit to live in us to enable us to live this new life—to think right, act right, and do right. We have a new life, so we are able to live accordingly. We have been cleared of all guilt! (See Romans 8:33.) We can come boldly to His throne and find mercy and grace, because we have a High Priest who understands what we are going through and what we feel (see Hebrews 4:15-16).

So what can we do when we are in this state of worry, anxiety, and or fright? Well, as mentioned previously, let's speak to ourselves in psalms, hymns, and spiritual songs.

What's the difference between psalms, hymns, and spiritual songs? Let's look at each.

WHAT ARE PSALMS?

Psalms are merely songs and prayers that were offered to God by His children. King David wrote most of the psalms throughout his lifetime, but they are relevant for us today as well. These psalms were to, and about, the one and only God, Creator of Heaven and earth, the absolute Sovereign of the universe. They are songs and prayers of praise, faith, hope, wisdom, frustration, and every human emotion we feel today.

There are 150 psalms in the Bible. Many people read *about* the psalms, but don't actually *read* the psalms. There are many that will encourage and strengthen our faith, and there are psalms we can actually sing and pray. The psalms do more than express our emotions. When we sing the psalms and believe in our hearts what we are singing, they shape our emotions. I'm not talking about standing and chanting in a monotone voice with your eyes rolled back in your head. I'm talking about knowing what we are singing and believing it in our heart. The psalms teach us to worship, and more importantly, they show us how to be honest before God.

If you are uncertain what to pray, just pour out your heart to your heavenly Father. Talk to Him, and then listen as He speaks to you through His Word, a poem, a song, or a friend. This is what David did over and over through the psalms. He was very bold when he spoke to the Lord. When he was discouraged, defeated, and afraid, David cried to the Lord.

For example, if you are overwhelmed, remember:

- God is a Father to the fatherless (see Psalm 68)
- He is our Helper (see Psalm 54)
- God satisfies the longing soul (see Psalm 107)
- He hears our cry in distress (see Psalm 120), and on and on.

After David cried to the Lord and complained, there was always praise, thanksgiving, and worship in David's communication with God. He knew that God could be trusted.

During one of the most difficult times in my life I turned to the Book of Psalms. I found so many promises that gave me great comfort and helped get me through a time of heartache and testing. There were times I felt like David when I wanted God to take revenge on someone who hurt my family and me. And then there were times of enormous grief over my unkindness and hard heart.

I must admit there are times when I still have some of those same emotions. I must turn to the One who can calm all my fears, the One who can tender my heart, the One who can comfort me during times of sorrow, the One who can encourage me when I am defeated, the One who can speak peace in times of turmoil. I don't think there will ever be a time when we don't need the truth and comfort of the psalms.

Beth Moore's book *Praying God's Word: Breaking Free from Spiritual Strongholds* is an excellent resource that can help us when we don't know what to pray. Sometimes we need help. That's why God sent His Holy Spirit to live in us, to help us, guide us, lead us, comfort and counsel us. In other words, Jesus wants to live His life through us. He gave Himself for us to give His life to us to live His life through us.

Psalm 121 has been one of my favorite chapters. It reminds me that my help comes from the Lord; He never slumbers or sleeps; He's my keeper; He will preserve my soul. In other words, He works the night shift. Ron Mehl wrote an inspiring book titled *God Works the Night Shift: Acts of Love Your Father Performs Even While You Sleep*. In the book, he reminds us of God's faithfulness to watch over His children.[4]

The following are two key verses that have meant a lot to me:

> *Let the words of my mouth and the meditation of my heart be acceptable in your sight, O Lord, my rock and my redeemer* (Psalm 19:14 ESV).

My mouth will speak the praise of the Lord, and let all flesh bless his holy name forever and ever (Psalm 145:21 ESV).

Psalm 100 is a great chapter to memorize, as it encourages us on worship and praise: *Make a joyful noise to the Lord, all the earth!*

Serve the Lord with gladness! Come into his presence with singing! Know that the Lord, he is God! It is he who made us, and we are His; we are his people, and the sheep of his pasture. Enter his gates with thanksgiving, and his courts with praise! Give thanks to him; bless his name! For the Lord is good; his steadfast love endures forever, and his faithfulness to all generations (ESV).

WHAT ARE HYMNS?

Hymns are simply songs of adoration and praise to our God. When I am discouraged or feeling overwhelmed, I take out my old hymnal and begin to read and sing the hymns. I sing out loud so I can hear myself. I sing songs such as "How Great Thou Art," "A Mighty Fortress is our God," "Amazing Grace," "When I Survey the Wondrous Cross," "There Is a Fountain," "How Deep the Father's Love for Us," and "The Love of God." These are some of the most cherished hymns of the Christian faith, and they have been around for hundreds of years for a reason.

I've been singing hymns since I was six years of age. My mother and two of my sisters, Mary and Carolyn, and I used to sing in church. Our pastor would say during the service, "Opal, you and your girls come sing for us." There were special songs we would sing. Two of the hymns I grew up singing were "Never Grow Old" and "Jesus Paid It All." In the song,

"Jesus Paid It All," there's a line that says it's God and God alone who can change the leper's spots. For years, I thought it was talking about changing a *leopard's* spots. I'm sure He can change the leopard's spots, but this beautiful hymn is not talking about changing animals, but the human heart:

> *Lord, now indeed I find*
> *Thy power, and Thine alone,*
> *Can change the leper's spots,*
> *And melt the heart of stone.*

As I grew older and began to understand the meaning of the hymns, they became very precious to me. One of the hymns that got me through some dark days was "On Christ the Solid Rock I Stand." Take a minute and reflect on the following words:

> *My hope is built on nothing less*
> *Than Jesus' blood and righteousness;*
> *I dare not trust the sweetest frame,*
> *But wholly lean on Jesus' name.*
> *On Christ, the solid Rock, I stand;*
> *All other ground is sinking sand.*
> *When darkness veils His lovely face,*
> *I rest on His unchanging grace;*
> *In every high and stormy gale*
> *My anchor holds within the veil.*
> *On Christ, the solid Rock, I stand;*
> *All other ground is sinking sand.*
> *His oath, His covenant, and blood*
> *Support me in the whelming flood;*
> *When every earthly prop gives way,*
> *He then is all my Hope and Stay.*
> *On Christ, the solid Rock, I stand;*
> *All other ground is sinking sand.*

When He shall come with trumpet sound,
Oh, may I then in Him be found,
Clothed in His righteousness alone,
Faultless to stand before the throne!
On Christ, the solid Rock, I stand;
All other ground is sinking sand.[5]

Now, if the message from that hymn doesn't encourage you as a Christian, there's something wrong!

WHAT ARE SPIRITUAL SONGS?

A spiritual song can be a praise chorus or a song of personal testimony. It might express the joy of one's salvation, revel in the grace of Christ, or exalt the greatness and power of God. So many of the songs of praise or choruses are the psalms or other Scriptures put to music. I believe God's Word is the greatest weapon we have as Christians to combat worry, anger, discouragement, and depression (see Psalm 149).

When my children were young and Paul was traveling, I would put Scripture to music to teach them the Word, the Truth. I needed His promises and encouragement as much as my children needed it. It's so easy to remember songs, so I would strum my guitar, as well as I could, and start singing Scriptures. It's amazing how I still remember so many verses that I put to music. One of those verses is Numbers 23:19: *"God is not a man, that He should lie; nor a son of man, that He should repent. Has He said, and will He not do? Or has He spoken, and will He not make it good?"*

*NOTE: Now is an excellent time to put this book down and sing a song of praise or a hymn and rejoice because of God's kindness, love, mercy, and grace. Find your favorite verses and start singing! Go ahead! You don't have to finish reading before you do this. *Do it now!*

Physical and Spiritual Anxiety

Why do we need to speak to ourselves in psalms, hymns, and spiritual songs? I believe our heavenly Father knows what worry or anxiety does to us in the physical realm, as well as the spiritual. Doctors say anxiety can cause a variety of ailments. For example, anxiety can cause a loss of appetite, muscle tension, headaches and insomnia, exhaustion, loss of hair, backache, and many other maladies. Anxiety can also cause panic attacks. If you are in a constant state of stress, it can lead to clinical depression.

Disease comes from two words: *dis* and *ease*, which is a lack of ease and harmony within the body. Many of our diseases are caused by anxiety, unforgiveness, fear, and stress. As mentioned previously, many diseases are caused by stress, but not all, so please don't think I'm blaming all disease on these four issues.

Worry is futile, and it's a sin! We aren't trusting in our Father who loves us and has promised to take care of every need we have. Does worry change what is causing your stress? No! Will you extend your life one more day by worrying? No! Can you change another person's heart by worrying? No!

What Is the Cure for Anxiety?

Jesus tells us in Matthew 6:25-34 (ESV):

> *Therefore I tell you, do not be anxious about your life, what you will eat or what you will drink, nor about your body, what you will put on. Is not life more than food, and the body more than clothing? Look at the birds of the air: they neither sow nor reap nor gather into barns, and yet your heavenly Father feeds them. Are you not of more*

value than they? And which of you by being anxious can add a single hour to his span of life? And why are you anxious about clothing? Consider the lilies of the field, how they grow: they neither toil nor spin, yet I tell you, even Solomon in all his glory was not arrayed like one of these. But if God so clothes the grass of the field, which today is alive and tomorrow is thrown into the oven, will he not much more clothe you, O you of little faith? Therefore do not be anxious, saying, "What shall we eat?"or "What shall we drink?" or "What shall we wear?" For the Gentiles seek after all these things, and your heavenly Father knows that you need them all. But seek first the kingdom of God and his righteousness, and all these things will be added to you. Therefore do not be anxious about tomorrow, for tomorrow will be anxious for itself. Sufficient for the day is its own trouble.

This about sums it up! I don't know about you, but I get the message. The cure for worry is *trust!* Trust in the Lord your God! Psalm 62:8 (ESV) declares, *"Trust in him at all times, O people; pour out your heart before him; God is a refuge for us."*

I believe there are some portions of Scripture we should read every day to remind us what Jesus taught. He wasn't just talking to hear Himself talk, He was giving instructions for godly living, faith living, and encouraging us to look to Him for our every need.

Sometimes we read God's Word and say, "WOW, that's good!" Yet we go on about our day not obeying what His Word tells us. If we don't put His truth and wisdom into practice in our everyday lives, it is not going to do us any good.

For instance, God says to love those who hate us, do good to those who do evil to us, bless those who curse us, and pray for those who despitefully use us. How often do we obey these commands? How often do we excuse ourselves by saying, "Well, they don't deserve my love or blessing." But these are not suggestions. They are commands! I don't know about you, but when I don't obey God, I feel condemned and guilty, and that's not the way a Christian should live. Conviction? Yes! Condemnation and guilt? No! We must trust and obey—abide by, act upon. Trust and obey! Trust and obey!

I am writing this book to Christian women who have the ability to make right choices. Why? Because God has given us His Holy Spirit to live within us to be our Helper in every area of our lives. When we say, "I can't love my husband! I can't stop overeating! I can't stop the adultery! I can't stop gossiping! I can't talk to my husband with kindness! I can't stop my mind from thinking on the wrong things!" what we are saying is we don't have the ability to make right choices. We need to be honest with ourselves and change the contraction to: I won't! I won't love my husband! I won't stop overeating! I won't stop the adultery! I won't quit gossiping! I won't take control of my mind!

God's Word says:

> *I can do all things through Christ who strengthens me* (Philippians 4:13).

> *For this reason I kneel before the Father, from whom every family in heaven and on earth derives its name. I pray that out of his glorious riches he may strengthen you with power through his Spirit in your inner being* (Ephesians 3:14-16 NIV).

> *Therefore most gladly I will rather boast in my infirmities, that the power of Christ may rest upon me* (2 Corinthians 12:9).

No temptation has overtaken you except such as is common to man; but God is faithful, who will not allow you to be tempted beyond what you are able, but with the temptation will also make the way of escape, that you may be able to bear it (1 Corinthians 10:13).

God has placed within us a special strength, power, divine nature, and ability. Charles Swindoll calls it "an extra inner reservoir of power that is more than a match for stuff life throws at us."[6]

There's a poem titled *Overheard in an Orchard* by Elizabeth Cheney. You may have heard it. The conversation between the robin and the sparrow may give insight to our anxiety. I have to remind myself of this every day. The poem is based on Matthew 6:26 that we read earlier, *"Look at the birds of the air, for they neither sow nor reap nor gather into barns; and yet your heavenly Father feeds them."*

> *Said the robin to the sparrow,*
> *"I should really like to know,*
> *Why these anxious human beings*
> *Rush about and worry so."*
> *Said the sparrow to the robin,*
> *"Friend I think that it must be,*
> *That they have no Heavenly Father,*
> *Such as cares for you and me."[7]*

ENDNOTES

1. Definition of anxiety; https://www.merriam-webster.com/dictionary/anxiety; accessed June 29, 2018.
2. John Edmund Haggai, *How to Win Over Worry* (Eugene, OR: Harvest House Publishing, 2001-2009), 67.

3. Max Lucado, "The Unspoken Source of Anxiety," April 2016; https://maxlucado.com/unspoken-source-anxiety/ (16); accessed June 29, 2018.

4. Author's note: I highly recommend purchasing Ron Mehl's book, *God Works the Night Shift: Acts of Love Your Father Performs Even While You Sleep.*

5. Edward Mote (1797-1874), *Baptist Hymnal: The Solid Rock* (Nashville, TN: Convention Press, 1975), 337.

6. Charles R. Swindoll, "Can't...or Won't? Part Two," www .insight.org/resources/daily-devotional/individual/can't -.-.-.-or-won't-part-two; accessed July 3, 2018.

7. Elizabeth Cheney, "Overheard in an Orchard," *Treasure Chest,* a ministry of Franklin Lakes Baptist Church; http:// golden-nuggets-flbc.blogspot.com/2013/02/poem-by -elizabeth-cheney-overheard-in.html; accessed December 20, 2018.

Chapter 4

Why Be Anxious When You Can Pray?

Do not be anxious about anything, but in everything by prayer and supplication with thanksgiving let your requests be made known to God. And the peace of God, which surpasses all understanding, will guard your hearts and your minds in Christ Jesus. Finally, brothers, whatever is true, whatever is honorable, whatever is just, whatever is pure, whatever is lovely, whatever is commendable, if there is any excellence, if there is anything worthy of praise, think about these things.
—Philippians 4:6-8 ESV

When Paul and I went through our struggles in the mid-1980s, I wanted to be a strong Christian. I wanted to live in victory regardless of the turmoil in my life. It was while I was waiting on the Lord, during this time of healing, that God showed me that I was carrying this burden of anxiety instead of letting Him carry it.

Come to me, all who labor and are heavy laden, and I will
give you rest. Take my yoke upon you, and learn from me,
for I am gentle and lowly in heart, and you will find rest
for your souls. For my yoke is easy, and my burden is light
(Matthew 11:28-30 ESV).

We women tend to carry stress, anxiety, cares, frustration, and all our worries on our shoulders, or in our bodies. This is why some women are stooped over as they go through life. We allow all of these things to weigh on us instead of letting God carry them. There are times when we don't realize we are doing this, as I just shared, but I do believe God will reveal this to us if we ask Him. Let's take our burdens to the Lord and leave them with Him.

In 1990, I started having severe pain in my back. There were times I couldn't sleep. During this time Paul and I traveled in our bus, and there were times the pain was so severe I had to get off of the road. I would stay with our son, Thom, in Oklahoma City, where he and Kelley lived. Sometimes I stayed for three weeks seeing chiropractors, massage therapists, and doctors. I had MRIs, but nothing showed up. I was so discouraged.

I knew this was hard on Paul, as he had to live with this sick and hurting woman. We prayed and prayed, but nothing changed. I sang the song, *He's an on-time God,* and would remind Him it was *time! What's the problem, God? I'm Your daughter. Can You hear me?* Paul would join me, and both of us fussed at God! We needed a miracle!

In 1995, Paul and I were going to a Bible conference in Augusta, Georgia. Our dear friend, Jack Taylor, was one of the speakers. One evening, Jack was praying for people who had been living with pain. I didn't go forward the first night even though I desperately needed God to heal me. However, the following night people began to give testimony about how God had healed them, so I asked Paul if he would go with me to have Jack pray for me. I told Jack I had been hurting for five years.

Jesus spoke a parable in Luke 18 that talks about a widow who came often before a judge. For a long time, the judge did nothing, but finally he thought to himself, *"Though I do not fear God nor regard man, yet because this widow troubles me I will avenge her, lest by her continual coming she weary me"* (Luke 18:4-5). I was going to be like this woman who wouldn't take no for an answer. When Jack prayed for me, I lost all of my strength. As I lay on the floor listening to my friend, Carrell Balltzglier, play a song, I knew God was healing me. The words of the song echo in my heart even today: "He is our peace, cast all your care [anxiety] on Him, for He cares for you, He is our peace, He is our peace."[1]

GOD THE HEALER

After the service, Paul and I, along with our son, Paul Edward, went to our bus for the night. Paul asked me if I was still hurting. I told him I was, but I told him I knew God healed me. We prayed and I went to bed and slept like a baby. The next morning, I got up completely healed! As we talked about my healing, I told Paul I believed that God had to disarm me in order to speak to my spirit.

We rely on our five senses every day—what we see, smell, taste, hear, and feel. God speaks to our spirit. As much as I knew how, I had cast my burdens and anxiety on Him. We prayed and asked God for healing for five years. We didn't give up. Paul would say, "Hon, we're getting older. We will have some aches and pains." I would tell him that I didn't believe God wanted me to live this way the rest of my life. Hallelujah! He answers prayer!

Throughout my years as a Christian, I have had many favorite Scripture passages, but one that's on the top of the list is Psalm 121. During a very difficult time in the 1980s, Paul and I received a letter from someone we thought was a friend. The letter was so discouraging that it just made my heart drop. He had sent it to many pastors around the country where Paul and I were going to minister. Some of the things that were said in the letter were true, but there were also many lies. I was so grateful that Paul was in Russia on a mission trip during this time. I was so disheartened that I didn't know how I would go back to the condo where our children were and not fall to pieces.

As I was driving back from the post office in Asheville, North Carolina, where we lived at the time, I saw beautiful, billowy clouds in the sky. They were high above the Blue Ridge Mountains, and as I looked up at those clouds, this promise came to my spirit:

> *I will lift up mine eyes to the hill—from whence comes my help? My help comes from the Lord, who made heaven and earth. He will not allow your foot to be moved; He who keeps you will not slumber* (Psalm 121:1-3).

I was so encouraged by this word from God—*my help comes from the Lord…He never sleeps.* He's aware of everything that happens in our lives.

During this time, I was reading the book *Trusting God* by Jerry Bridges. That evening God gave me two more verses that have been the mainstay in my life. Lamentations 3:37-38 (NIV) says, *"Who can speak and have it happen if the Lord has not decreed it? Is it not from the mouth of the Most High that both calamities and good things come?"*

Friend, let me tell you, these verses encouraged my heart and got me through the night. I realized that no one can say a thing or write a letter unless God allows it, so it must be for my good and His glory that it was written. Why? I don't know, but I know I can trust God in everything that happens in my life. He's in charge! He allows, permits, or directs everything that happens in this universe.

In Philippians 4:6-8 (cited at the beginning of this chapter) when the Lord said, *"but in everything by prayer,"* I had to know what He meant. I thought, *Okay, Lord, what do You mean by everything?* He said, *"Everything."* Everything means all, all things, each thing, every little thing, sum, the works, total, the whole enchilada, all-inclusive, including all categories, and including all members. I think that pretty much covers everything! But how? How can I truly *not* be anxious? By prayer and supplication! It seems so simple, yet so hard.

Prayer in this passage from Philippians 4 simply means worship, and supplication means petition. I've heard it said that prayer is preoccupation with our needs; praise is preoccupation with our blessings; and worship is preoccupation with Jesus. So, I would say that we should worship before we ask or petition Him for anything. Prayer is dialogue, not monologue.

Billy Graham said:

> Prayer is spiritual communication between man and God, a two-way relationship in which man should not only talk to God but also listen to Him. Prayer to God is like a child's conversation with his father. It is natural for a child to ask his father for the things he needs. When you receive Christ into your heart, you become a child of God and have the privilege of talking to Him in prayer at any time about anything. The Christian life is a personal relationship to God through Jesus Christ. And best of all, it is a relationship that will last for all eternity.[2]

Driving seems to be a great time for me to pray. I can talk to the Lord out loud with no one around and pour out my heart to Him. Before I get out of bed in the morning is another time for prayer. All day long there are times when we can talk to our Father. We don't have to be in a certain position, even though there are times when I believe we will fall on our face before God. It's not the position of our body—it's the condition of our hearts that He sees.

We read throughout the Bible about the different positions people took when they were talking to the Lord. King David humbly sought God while sitting (2 Samuel 7:18); Solomon stood before the altar of the Lord and spread out his hands toward Heaven (1 Kings 8:22). Apostle Paul exhorted that people pray with holy hands lifted, without anger or disputing (1 Timothy 2:8). As mentioned previously, it's the condition of our hearts not the position of our body that is important. We can pray while we are sitting, standing, kneeling, eyes closed or wide open. I can't remember reading in the Bible where we should close our eyes and bow our heads when we pray.

WORSHIP

Because prayer includes worship, what is worship? Worship is to honor with extravagant love and extreme submission.

> Our worship must be toward the one who is worthy simply because of his identity as the Omnipotent, Omniscient, and Omnipresent One, and not just because God is wealthy and able to meet our needs and answer our prayers. We must focus our practice of worship on the worthiness of God and not his wealthiness.[3]

I believe when we rehearse to God, who He is, He is pleased and worshipped. God is Lord, King, Redeemer, Shepherd,

Mighty God, Healer, Bread of Life, Deliver, Wonderful Counselor, Prince of Peace, Master, All Sufficient One, our Provider and Friend. And, the list goes on and on.

Rick Warren wrote the following about true worship:

> After spending eleven chapters in the book of Romans explaining God's incredible grace to us, Paul urges us to fully surrender our lives to God in worship: "So then, my friends, because of God's great mercy to us...offer yourselves a living sacrifice to God, dedicated to his service and pleasing to him. This is the true worship you should offer. (Romans 12:1 TEV). True worship—bringing God pleasure—happens when you give yourself completely to God. Notice the first and last words of that verse are the same: offer.[4]

Supplication is petitioning God for our needs. God's Word tells us over and over to come to Him

> John 14:14: *"If you ask anything in My name, I will do it."*
> Matthew 7:7: *"Ask, and it will be given you; seek, and you will find; knock, and it will be opened to you."*
> Ephesians 3:20: *"Now to him who is able to do exceeding abundantly above all that we ask or think, according to the power that works in us."*
> James 1:5: *"If any of you lacks wisdom, let him ask of God, who gives to all liberally and without reproach, and it will be given to him."*

I believe prayer is more for us than for God. After all, He knows what we have need of before we ask. He knows the thoughts of our heart before we even think them!

> *For the word of God is living and powerful, and sharper than any two-edged sword, piercing even to the*

division of soul and spirit, and of joints and marrow, and is a discerner of the thoughts and intents of the heart (Hebrews 4:12).

In the Book of Luke, it is said many times that Jesus knew the thoughts of their hearts. Yes, He knows our thoughts, yet He says ask. I don't believe anything is too small; after all, He said in *everything* by prayer and supplication.

Before we left Gretchen at the university, we were in the dorm room helping her get settled. I left her a devotional book by Charles Swindoll titled *Come Before Winter.* I wrote in the front of the book: *Don't think! Don't hope! Don't wish! PRAY!* So often we spend our time thinking and wishing rather than really praying and talking to our Father. If our children just thought about things that they need or want and never came to us and asked for them, how would we know their heart's desires? Yes, God knows our thoughts before we even think them, but He told us to ask, seek, and knock!

For years, I was afraid to share my heart with the Lord, as though He didn't already know. *Oh, I don't want to say it out loud, God may hear me!* HELLO? Listen, friend, we aren't going to surprise Him. He already knows! Tell Him! Talk to Him, and let Him know that you trust Him with your life. The same way we love to hear from our children, God loves to hear from His.

SINCERITY

As a young girl, I was raised in church. I felt like I had to hold my hands the right way, bow my head, bend my knees, and say the right words when beginning a prayer or else God wouldn't hear me. Maybe I learned this from my dad. I used to dread when the pastor would call on him to pray at the end of a service. I would think, *Oh no, we'll never get out of church.*

He prayed what seemed like an hour. I think he was trying to catch up on his praying when he got to church. Don't get me wrong, he was a very good father and loved Jesus. And I'm sure he was very sincere in his prayers, but as a young child it was very annoying.

In Matthew chapter 6, Jesus talks about prayer. He said we shouldn't be like the hypocrites who pray while standing on the street corners where they can be seen by others. When they do this, that's the only reward they get—accolades from people. How empty!

Jesus said we should go find a place where we can be alone when we pray. God knows and sees and will reward us. Then, Jesus goes on to give us the Lord's Prayer. This does not mean we pray this word for word like a rote prayer. When we pray, let's understand what we are praying. I believe we acknowledge God for who He is, our Father. This is a personal relationship with our Father who loves us and gave His only begotten Son to die for us so that we might have abundant life. He is holy, set apart. There's none like Him.

You get the idea. I'm not saying don't pray the Lord's Prayer, but just don't make it empty phrases that we've memorized and has become so familiar that we just pray it to be praying like it's our duty! No, it's our privilege to pray. We have to pray with our eyes on God, not on our difficulties.

Paul and I fly a lot. As we are flying over different cities and countries, I look out the window and realize there are millions of people down below. I think to myself, *Lord, how can You hear the prayers of millions and millions of your people? How can one person affect a situation through prayer? Is my prayer really heard and attended to?* I don't know about you, but this boggles my mind. Oh, I believe He hears and answers. Even if just one person is praying for that specific request, I believe our God hears. I also believe it encourages the person who asked for prayer, knowing someone on this huge round ball called Earth cares—cares enough to call upon the Lord on their behalf.

When someone asks that we pray for him or her or for something that is going on in the person's life, I usually pray as soon as I'm asked. It's so easy to forget as the day goes on. Our lives are so busy that other things crowd out our promise to pray. And remember, we pray, but God intervenes and answers the way He wants, not the way we want.

Lisa Simmons is a friend who has a great talent for writing poems, just like my hubby. I asked if she had a poem on prayer. She just happened to have one and I want to share it with you, as it speaks volumes. It's very convicting, as at times I get too busy to stop and talk with my Father.

Hope to Hear from You Soon

I waited by your bed today
I thought you'd get up and pray.
But you got dressed and walked away.
Hope to hear from you soon.
And while you drove to get to work
The man you honked at…called a jerk
If you only knew the news he heard,
Hope to hear from you soon.
You sat behind your busy desk
Your assistant came…looked distressed,
You didn't ask about her tests,
Hope to hear from you soon.
Now you're home; the kids are fed
It's 8:00; tuck them in bed,
A little prayer-like poem is said,
Hope to hear from you soon.
As you lie down to go to sleep

You start to pray, can't seem to keep
Your mind on Me; I start to weep,
Hope to hear from you soon.
Then life begins to spiral down
You seek my help as you drown
And even though I've been around
I'm glad to finally hear the sound
Of your voice though in distress,
"Please help me, Lord; my life's a mess."
All the times I offered rest but never heard
"Lord, I am blessed."
But still I'm here, have no fear
Your Father's near.And I will answer you soon.[5]

ENDNOTES

1. Maranatha! Music, Lyrics, "He Is Our Peace," https://www .musixmatch.com/lyrics/Maranatha-Music/He-Is-Our-Peace; accessed July 10, 2018.

2. Billy Graham Evangelistic Association, "What is Prayer?" https://billygraham.org/answer/what-is-prayer/; accessed July 10, 2018.

3. Delesslyn A. Kennebrew, "What is true worship?" ChristianityToday.com; https://www.christianitytoday.com/ biblestudies/bible-answers/spirituallife/what-is-true-worship .html; accessed July 10, 2018).

4. Rick Warren, *The Purpose Driven Life* (Grand Rapids, MI: Zondervan Publishing, 2002), 78.

5. Lisa Simmons, *I Would Have Said Yes: A Family's Journey with Autism* (Westbow Press, 2012); https. (This book is available to purchase on amazon.com.)

Chapter 5

In Everything Give Thanks

*Do not be anxious about anything, but in every
situation, by prayer and petition, with thanksgiving,
present your requests to God. And the peace of God,
which transcends all understanding, will guard
your hearts and your minds in Christ Jesus. Finally,
brothers and sisters, whatever is true, whatever is
noble, whatever is right, whatever is pure, whatever
is lovely, whatever is admirable—if anything is
excellent or praiseworthy—think about such things.*
—Philippians 4:6-8 NIV

I BELIEVE THERE IS ALWAYS SOMETHING WE CAN BE THANK-
ful for, no matter our situation. When our lives seem to be
falling apart, we can be thankful for salvation; we will live
with Christ for eternity. We can be thankful for God's unconditional love. What we need to do is turn our hearts and
minds away from our circumstances, and turn our eyes toward
home—Heaven.

We need to be like Daniel in the den of lions. I gave our
son, Thom, a picture of Daniel standing in the den of lions.

Daniel had his hands behind his back in complete surrender. He wasn't looking at the lions but gazing out of a small opening with his eyes toward Heaven. He was focused on his Lord, not the lions. No one really knows what he was thinking, but I'm sure he knew he couldn't do anything about his dire situation. He did serve a God who could do something. We need to be like Daniel and focus on our Lord, not our problems.

When I look at the night sky or watch the gorgeous sunrise each morning, my heart is full of gratitude and thanksgiving—for surely the heavens declare the glory of God. There's an old hymn I used to sing that was written by John W. Peterson. As I was thinking about things to be grateful and thankful for, I replayed this stanza in my heart:

> *My Father is omnipotent*
> *And that you can't deny;*
> *A God of might and miracles;*
> *'Tis written in the sky.*

> *It took a miracle to put the stars in place;*
> *It took a miracle to hang the world in space.*
> *But when He saved my soul,*
> *Cleansed and made me whole,*
> *It took a miracle of love and grace!*[1]

This is definitely something for which we should be grateful. He cleansed and made us whole. We are complete. He saved us by His grace.

There aren't many mornings when I wake up and not thank God for letting me wake up to a brand-new day. Each day I'm thankful for Paul, my children, my grandchildren, and my great-grandsons. I continue to offer praise for my brother and sister and their spouses, my friends, and my enemies. I am especially thankful to my heavenly Father for letting me get out of bed and see the beautiful sunrise and sunset. I am thankful for the smell of the sweet flowers in my garden, giving me health, letting me smell the wonderful breakfast I'm cooking, and giving me a sound mind! There are so many other reasons, too numerous to mention, to be grateful to our Father.

THANKSGIVING AND GRATITUDE

I can remember one particular night, when Paul and I lived and traveled in our bus, that I woke up to check on something. All of a sudden, my heart was overwhelmed by God's goodness. I remember getting back under our heavy comforter with thanksgiving and gratitude filling my heart to overflowing. It was one of those times when I didn't know how to express all that I was feeling. However, I began to thank Him for letting my heart continue to beat. I realized so completely that He only had to remove His hand, and my heart would stop. There were no words to adequately express my love and desire to love and please Him. However, I knew He knew how grateful I was for His love and care for me.

As we read the psalms, we realize that David was a man full of thanksgiving and praise to his Lord, even though he experienced many trials and heartache. That's why we have the psalms. They are David's cries, frustration, fear, and even anger—as well as his praise and worship of his heavenly Father. He wasn't afraid to pour out his heart.

The psalms remind us of so many things for which we should be thankful. We give thanks to Him because He is good. His love is unconditional. He cares for us. He watches over us. He protects us. We thank God because He redeemed us. Again, in the psalms, we thank God because He gives us good gifts, He establishes justice, and He shows mercy. The Bible has a whole catalog of things for which we ought to give thanks.

We give thanks because it's God's will for us. First Thessalonians 5:18 says, *"In everything give thanks; for this is the will of God in Christ Jesus for you."*

Growing up attending an Independent Baptist Church, my concept of God was a huge man in Heaven with a big stick waiting to conk me on the head when I made a mistake. I know that's not what was preached, but that was what I thought. How could I be thankful, or trust a god like that? How could I turn my life over to a god like that? How sad to think I viewed my heavenly Father in this way. And, it is unfortunate that some people see their heavenly Father the same way as their earthly father. We shouldn't compare our earthly father—whether he was good or bad—to our heavenly Father.

First John 4:7-8 declares that God is love. He demonstrated His love by sending His only begotten Son into the world that we might live through Him. We love Him because He first loved us.

The word "love" is often used without real meaning. We say things like I love my dog, I love my house, I love my car, I love my husband, and I love my hair. We seem to put everything and everyone in the same level of love. We need to define the kind of love we are talking about when we say we love something or someone. Do we love our husband with the same type of love as our car? No! Do we love our animals with the same kind of love as our children? No. Then, let's define the kind of love we have for people and things.

In the Bible, there are three types of love—*agape, phileo,* and *eros.* Let's look at each more closely.

Agape love is unconditional. It's about sacrifice, as well as giving. This is the kind of love God has for us. God demonstrated His love by giving Jesus, His only begotten Son, to pay the penalty for our sins. Agape is committed and chosen love. This is the kind of love we have for our families.

Phileo love is an affectionate, warm, and tender platonic love. It makes you desire friendship with someone.

I found the following description of phileo love; I love how the writer makes it so clear:

> The two words, agapáō and philéō are best understood when one carefully analyzes the conversation that the risen Christ had with the Apostle Peter in John 21:15-19. Peter confessed that though he fell short of the supreme and sacrificial love of Christ (agapáō which is a response to His love), he was His real friend (philéo) and wanted to make the interests of Christ his own interests. Since that was the case, the Lord entrusted Peter with the shepherding of His flock. In sum, phileo is the love that has tender affections for another, but it always expects a response. It is the "friendship" type love.[2]

Eros love describes something that is simply an emotional and sensual love. Eros is the kind of love that wants to satisfy physical emotions; a shallow form of love to satisfy self rather than another. Paul has had guys and gals tell him that they have fallen in love with someone who's not their spouse. He says to them that he's sure they do love them, but what kind of love is it? Is it agape love, the kind God gives? Or is it eros love—a sensual, sexual, selfish love that wants to try to satisfy the lust of the flesh? We should have agape love, God's love, for everyone. However, eros love for someone else's spouse is not agape love.

When I think about these three types of love, I am so thankful that our Father loves us with an undying love—agape love. His love never ends, no matter how we act. He is committed to us. One of my absolute favorite verses is found in Second Timothy 2:13: *"If we are faithless, He remains faithful; He cannot deny Himself."*

My dear friend, let us practice being thankful. Wake up each morning with a psalm of praise and thanksgiving. Our day will go so much better than if we wake up growling! I'm sure you've heard the saying, "What if you woke up today with only the things you thanked God for yesterday?" That's a scary thing!

When I was a young girl in Vacation Bible School, I used to sing a little chorus that was written by Seth and Bessie Sykes in the 1800s. I really didn't understand or think about the message at that time. However, it blesses me every time I sing it because I understand it's meaning now:

> *Thank You, Lord, for saving my soul,*
> *Thank You, Lord, for making me whole;*
> *Thank You, Lord, for giving to me*
> *Thy great salvation so rich and free.*[3]

Let's make a choice every day to find at least five things to be thankful for and verbally thank God for each. Why not write them down in a journal? You'll be surprised, as you get older, how many things you forget. But when you look back over your journal in a few years, you will see how faithful God has been.

I love this portion of Scripture from Timothy:

> *I thank him who has given me strength, Christ Jesus our Lord, because he judged me faithful, appointing me to his service, though formerly I was a blasphemer, persecutor, and insolent opponent. But I received mercy because I had acted ignorantly in unbelief, and the grace of our Lord overflowed for me with the faith and love that are in Christ Jesus* (1 Timothy 1:12-14 ESV).

If nothing else, we can be thankful for God's undying love for us, His forgiveness, His faithfulness, His patience, His longsuffering, His kindness, His mercy, and His gift of salvation.

When Paul and I were in evangelism, we traveled through many towns around the United States and Canada. As we were driving through a small town in Louisiana, I was watching all the people walking along the sidewalk. All of a sudden, my heart was overwhelmed with thanksgiving. I turned to Paul and said, "Out of all the people in the world, God chose me to be His daughter. Why me? Why did He open my eyes and heart? Why did He give me faith to trust Him? Why did He choose to put His truth into my heart?" My questioning reminded me of Ephesians 1:4, *"just as he chose us in Him before the foundation of the world, that we should be holy and without blame before Him in love."* I don't know why He chose me, but I am full of praise and thanksgiving for His mercy and grace toward me.

We all want our children to be grateful and thankful for what we give them and what we do for them. Well, our heavenly Father wants us to be grateful and thankful for all He does for us. When we give a gift to someone, it's a joy to hear the person say, "Thank you." If someone is not grateful or thankful for a gift I've given them, I'm not too anxious to provide another gift.

Paul and I are so different when it comes to thanking a person for a gift. I say, "Thank you, I really appreciate it." Paul thanks them over and over and over and over again. The next time he sees them, he thanks them yet again. We've laughed many times over the different ways of thanking someone. The important thing is to say thank you and be grateful. God loves a cheerful giver. Give thanks!

ENDNOTES

1. John W. Peterson (1921-2006), "It Took a Miracle," https://hymnary.org/text/my_father_is_omnipotent; accessed July 18, 2018.

2. Zodhiates, "Love-Phileo (Greek Word Study)," An Exegetical Commentary on First Corinthians One; Precept Austin; http://www.preceptaustin.org/love-phileo; accessed July 18, 2018.

3. Seth and Bessie Sykes, "Thank You, Lord," HymnPod; http://www.hymnpod.com/2009/01/27/thank-you-lord/; accessed July 18, 2018.

Chapter 6

Present Your Requests to God

*Do not be anxious about anything, but in every
situation, by prayer and petition, with thanksgiving,
present your requests to God. And the peace of God,
which transcends all understanding, will guard
your hearts and your minds in Christ Jesus. Finally,
brothers and sisters, whatever is true, whatever is
noble, whatever is right, whatever is pure, whatever
is lovely, whatever is admirable—if anything is
excellent or praiseworthy—think about such things.*
—PHILIPPIANS 4:6 8 NIV

I F WE REALLY WANT SOMETHING, OUR REQUESTS SHOULD BE
to the One who can do something about our need or situation.
God says we are to ask—not think, hope, or wish—*ask!*

For many years when I prayed, my request was for God to
make me the woman of God and Paul the man of God He
desired us to be and that we wanted to be. But as God began
to work things out for His glory and my good, I wanted to run.
I wanted an easier avenue of growth, one that wouldn't humble me or bring embarrassment to our family. I didn't like

what He was doing to work this out in my life. I prayed, "Surely, Father, You could use something that would be easier or more acceptable to society and even the Christian world." But as I look back through the years, I am so thankful for everything God allowed in my life to help me grow and mature, as now I have a softer heart for the hurting, no matter the hurt.

Have you ever requested of the Lord to make you kinder? I tell you, my friend, He will put the "not so kind people" in your life in order to answer your request. And when you ask God for patience, you can certainly anticipate that He will answer you. But once again, His answer may not be in the way you expect. James put it this way when said, *"Consider it pure joy, my brothers and sisters, whenever you face trials of many kinds, because you know that the testing of your faith produces perseverance. Let perseverance finish its work so that you may be mature and complete, not lacking anything"* (James 1:2-4 NIV).

Pastor Ed Richards wrote:

> Trials, sufferings, persecution and other times of tribulation will enter into our lives, but it is not a time to lose courage. Paul wrote, "And not only this, but we even glory in the tribulations, KNOWING that the tribulation works patience;" God often sends testing that His children may learn to look to Him, to trust Him more completely, to lean heavily upon Him and not upon their own strength. Tests of faith will produce patience.[1]

So be careful what you ask for!

When you say, "Lord, I need to love people like You love them," I'm sure you will meet the most unlovable people. It's easy for me to love those who love me, and I'm sure you can say the same. That's easy for everyone. The Bible says, *"If you love those who love you, what credit is that to you? For even sinners love those who love them. And if you do good to those who do good to you, what credit is that to you? For even sinners do the same"* (Luke 6:32-33).

We don't always get what we request of the Lord, but without a doubt, we receive everything *He* knows we need. We can trust Him. He knows what we have need of before we ask: *"For your Father knows what things you have need of before you ask Him"* (Matthew 6:8).

RUNNING FROM GOD

When I was pregnant with our son Thom, Paul Edward was two years old. I had gained a lot of weight, so it wasn't easy to get around. One day the children and I were out in the front yard playing. I told Paul Edward to do something. He decided he didn't want to do it, so I headed toward him. When he saw me coming, he took off running. To say it was hard for me to run is an understatement. Even at his young age, Paul Edward knew he shouldn't run away from me. But, once he started running, even though he knew he would get caught and get disciplined, he continued to run until I finally caught him.

I believe we do this same thing at times in our Christian walk. Why do we run from Him or refuse to talk to Him? God convicts us about something in our lives or speaks to our heart about doing something, but we don't want to change. We don't want to be inconvenienced, so we start running from Him. We try everything in the world to drown out His voice. We stay away from reading His Word. We don't pray. We may even stop going to church. Deep in our heart, we know God has the "reach" on us, but we run anyway. Eventually, we get tired of running. The amazing truth is, God can catch us any time He wants.

We have a loving, heavenly Father who wants to take us in His arms and embrace us with His love. But there are times when He lets us run until we are so desperate that we are over-joyed when He catches us. When we are willing to say, "Not my will but Your will be done. Whatever You desire for my life, I am submitting to Your calling." Praise God He never gives up on us.

There are many verses that tell us He is longsuffering, gracious, and full of mercy. Jesus bids us to ask, seek, and knock:

> *Ask, and it will be given to you; seek and you will find; knock and the door will be opened to you. For everyone who asks receives; the one who seeks finds; and to the one who knocks, the door will be opened. Which of you, if your son asks for bread, will give him a stone? Or if he asks for a fish, will give him a snake? If you, then, though you are evil, know how to give good gifts to your children, how much more will your Father in heaven give good gifts to those who ask him!* (Matthew 7:7-11 NIV)

We read this admonition again in Mark, Luke, and John... *ask!* Do I believe we should ask selfishly to heap blessings on ourselves? No. But I do believe we can ask according to God's will. Prayers like: *"Lord, I need You to forgive me." "Lord, I need Your Word to guide me into all truth." "Lord, I need You to help me love my enemies."* To be guided by the truth, we have to know the truth. God's Word is truth! (See 1 Timothy 2:4; John 17:17.) In 1973, Paul and I moved our family from Victoria, Texas, to Shamrock, Texas. The night we arrived in Shamrock, we met two wonderful families. For the next year, Paul would be traveling with an evangelist, who was also from Shamrock. This was the place to be. So, here I am, twenty-five years of age, very far from my family, with virtually no friends. I have a baby, a three-year-old, and a five-year-old. And, to top it off, Thom, our youngest son, who was only a year old, was very sick with a cold!

The day after we arrived in Shamrock, we moved about a mile from town, we unpacked the truck and put the boxes in the apartment. Then Paul drove off, leaving me without transportation. There were no cell phones; it was snowing; and I had a sick little guy with a high fever. I had no idea where anything was because we hadn't unpacked any boxes, and he needed medicine!

I needed help! It was too late to call the new friends I had just met. I felt so alone. Who could I call? Who could I turn to during this time? There was one place I could go for help! My request was to the Lord. I laid my hands on Thom and simply asked God to take away the fever. Immediately, it was gone! God heard my cry and answered my prayer. He knew I was desperate; *"Present your requests to God."*

I've had a poem in the front of an old Bible for many years. There is no telling how many times I've read it! It reminds me to take my requests—burdens, trouble, wants, needs, etc.—to the Lord and leave them with Him.

> *As children bring their broken toys with tears*
> *for us to mend,*
> *I brought my broken dreams to God,*
> *because He was my friend.*
> *But, then, instead of leaving Him*
> *in peace to work alone,*
> *I hung around and tried to help,*
> *with ways that were my own.*
> *At last I snatched them back and cried,*
> *"How can you be so slow?"*
> *"My child," He said, "What could I do?*
> *You never did let go."*
> —Author Unknown

Oh, I know there are times we need to talk to each other about situations in our lives. After all, Paul and I are counselors, and people tell us about their struggles and situations. I believe there are times we need to share our burdens so that our "Christian family" will know how to pray for us.

But, this doesn't mean we should constantly be sharing our troubles with everyone we meet. We don't want people hiding from us because they don't want to hear our troubles one more time. There's an old song that says, *"Take your burdens to the Lord and leave them there."* In other words, leave them with your Father...not with your friends.

Now, if a friend comes to us and is burdened down with guilt and shame and needs someone to talk to and is repentant, what should we do? God's Word says:

> *Brothers, if anyone is caught in any transgression, you who are spiritual should restore him in a spirit of gentleness. Keep watch on yourself, lest you too be tempted. Bear one another's burdens, and so fulfill the law of Christ.* (Galatians 6:1-2 ESV).

The word "burdens" in this passage is talking about a load or weight that someone is carrying because of a wrong choice. In other words—sinning. The word "transgression" means sin, error, fault, offense, trespass, and wrongdoing! When people are repentant, we should help restore them, bear their burdens, help them through their struggles. A *spiritual* person will do this, at least that's what I read! Think about it for a second. If a friend should come to you in repentance, would the person find condemnation or forgiveness? It's amazing how easy it is to forgive someone we don't know. But a friend who has broken trust? A friend who has deceived us? Someone we look up to? Would we be one of the *"you who are spiritual"* talked about in this Scripture passage? Or, would we try to preach to them to let them know how severely they disappointed us? A good question to ponder.

Let me ask you again. Have you requested of the Lord to teach you to be more forgiving? Have you requested of Him to make you a true friend? Have you prayed for God to make you the godly woman you desire to be? You can be confident that He will answer your requests but not in the way you think He should.

I love the way Amy Rees Anderson put it:

> We are so blessed to have such an amazing Heavenly Father who loves us enough to give us what we need and what He knows will bring us the greatest joy and happiness. If it weren't for Him we would all end up settling for what we thought our lives could be, and our lives would end up being nothing compared to the masterpiece God knew they could be. That's why we have to trust Him. We have to do all we can in our power to get the things we want and then trust the outcome completely…after all we can do we must let go and trust God…have faith![2]

As mentioned previously in this chapter, I didn't like what God used to bring Paul and me to repentance and change, but I am thankful He did. Our loving Father will always give us His best when we leave the choice up to Him. He will make us vessels that are pleasing to Him. Trust and obey, there's no other way!

ENDNOTES

1. Ed Richards, *Living Faith* (Orlando, FL: Golden Rule Book Press, 1986), 26.
2. Amy Rees Anderson, "God Intends to Give Us What We Need, Not What We Now Think We Want"; http://www .amyreesanderson.com/blog; accessed September 18, 2018.

Chapter 7

I Have Peace Like a River

Do not be anxious about anything, but in everything by prayer and supplication with thanksgiving let your requests be made known to God. And the peace of God, which surpasses all understanding, will guard your hearts and your minds in Christ Jesus. Finally, brothers, whatever is true, whatever is honorable, whatever is just, whatever is pure, whatever is lovely, whatever is commendable, if there is any excellence, if there is anything worthy of praise, think about these things.
—Philippians 4:6-8 ESV

Reading what the apostle Paul wrote about having the *"peace of God"* might lead us to say, "It's easy for Paul to say this extraordinary peace of God is available because he doesn't know what I've been through." Really? We need to remember that Paul was writing his letter from prison to the Christians at Philippi. He wasn't sure he was going to make it out alive. Yet he had peace knowing that no matter what was happening around him, he was going to trust God. He knew God was in control of the situation.

Being thrown in prison like a criminal was because he was sharing the gospel. As far as Paul was concerned, whether he lived or died, he would win. He said, *"For to me to live is Christ, and to die is gain"* (Philippians 1:21 ESV). He could rest in the promise that God would never leave him or forsake him (see Hebrews 13:5-6).

"Peace" in this passage means rest and tranquility. When Paul wrote his letter, the church at Philippi was suffering persecution. Paul was encouraging them to trust in God and not become unsettled, anxious, or worried. How could he say that? Simple, they belonged to the Lord! He encouraged them to pray instead of worrying about their circumstances. No matter their situation, they were to pray and give thanks. God's promise in Isaiah 26:3 (NIV) says, *"You will keep in perfect peace those whose minds are steadfast, because they trust in you."*

I looked up some pictures that represent peace and was amazed at the different concepts of peace that people have. Most all of the pictures were of serene places, doves, hearts, the peace sign, flowers, animals, children, and boats on a calm sea.

Years ago, there was a contest for artists to draw their concept of peace. There were many contestants. The second-place winner was a picture of a peaceful scene of a meadow with the wind softly blowing causing the grass to sway in the breeze. There was a huge oak tree in the middle of the field, and a young boy was sitting under the tree. There was a small pond right near the tree. The young boy's faithful dog was lying beside him with his head in the little boy's lap. The boy was holding a fishing pole with the line in the water and the bobber bouncing up and down with ripples moving slowing from the bobber. The scene was titled *Peace*.

The artist who won the first prize painted a picture of a tempestuous sea with high waves brought on by the wind.

Foam gathered on the huge waves and nestled inside one of the waves, down in one of the corners of the wave was a bird with his head tucked under one wing, sound asleep. This is when we truly need the peace that God gives—when we are smack dab in the middle of our storms.

It's easy to experience peace when things are going great in our lives. However, in life, there are going to be storms, whether we like it or not. We can experience the peace that passes all understanding because we are safe in the arms of Jesus; resting in Him. Isaiah 54:10 (NIV) says:

> *"Though the mountains be shaken and the hills be removed, yet my unfailing love for you will not be shaken nor my covenant of peace be removed," says the Lord, who has compassion on you.*

PEACE IN TOUGH TIMES

In the mid-1980s, Paul and I went through one of the toughest times in our marriage. There's no doubt Paul trusted Jesus in 1971 and was a changed man. I know, because I live with him. However, as the years went by, he took his eyes off of Jesus and started looking at men and their failures. Paul began to travel a lot. Great doors of opportunity were opening. He was preaching on national platforms with some noted pastors. Invitations began to pour in for him to hold revival meetings. He has said, "Too much too soon can give a man a false sense of where those blessings come from." God's Word is true: *"Pride goes before destruction, a haughty spirit before a fall* (Proverbs 16:18 NIV).

In 2011, Paul and I wrote a book titled *Get Married, Stay Married*. The following random quotes are excerpted from pages 100-106.

Paul writing in his own words:

As you may know from experience, being a Christian doesn't automatically make you a better person, but it is the living day in and day out, overcoming selfishness to be more like Jesus that creates change. No matter how a person came to God, when he or she lets other things cloud their daily walk, it won't be long before they lose sight of where God is leading them and head off in the wrong direction once again. If there are no course corrections along this path, it is just as natural for a Christian to end up shipwrecked along a rocky shore as it is for anyone else.

Temptation still had a beachhead in my life, and at the dawn of the 1980s, feeling I had arrived to some degree as a man of God, I started giving into little things my selfish nature wanted. Bitterness, anger and frustration increasingly bubbled up in my life and Billie was often the focus of these emotions. While everything looked good on the outside to those around us, inside I had built a barrier between Billie and me and had hardened my heart toward God to the point that my desires to please myself were smothering my desire to please Him.

As a favor to a friend, I was counseling his daughter on her marriage. I accept full complete responsibility for the adultery that followed between us; my choice, my failure, and my becoming a stumbling block to another person. God would ultimately use this event to bring me to the end of my struggle and begin a new work in me.

For months, I was unable to tell Billie or my family what had happened, but the issue came to a head later when I received one of the most heartbreaking letters of my life. A board had been formed to ask for my resignation as Staff Evangelist from the church. I did so knowing it would have been very difficult under the circumstances to be restored in that church. I truly came to the end of myself that day and knew I had to tell Billie what happened.[1]

Paul flew me to Colorado where he was preaching a revival meeting to tell me about his adultery. He begged me not to leave him. I told him it was not even a thought in my mind… we would work through this. It was a difficult time, to say the least. Yet, I knew we would work through it with God's help.

I believe one of the hardest things to do, at this time, was to leave our home in Louisiana. I thought I would live my life out in that house. We raised our children there, and the memories were abundant. However, God knew what our future was, so He was moving us on to our new adventure.

We packed a big truck and headed to North Carolina—to who knew what! What did the future hold for us? Would we have a ministry? Did God really care what we were going through in our lives? As we were driving toward our future destiny, this Scripture came to mind: *"Do not be anxious about anything."* I thought, *Lord, can You see what's going on down here? How can I not be anxious or troubled?*

As I read the rest of the passage, I understood the promise: *"…peace that surpasses all understanding…whatever is true, honorable, just, pure, lovely, commendable, worthy of praise, think about these things"!* This promise was a revelation to me. I had never put those verses together. I believe this was when I began to understand the importance of not *listening* to myself but *speaking* to myself. Speaking to myself? Speaking what? Ephesians 5:19 (NIV) says, *"speaking to one another with psalms, hymns, and songs from the Spirit. Sing and make music from your heart to the Lord."* If we are to speak to one another in this manner, there's no doubt we will be counseling ourselves at the same time and being encouraged by our own words.

We must think on the right things if we are going to have peace that passes all understanding. I really couldn't understand why I had such peace, even though I was devastated and not sure what the future held. As I read this portion of Scripture, I understood! I made up my mind not to think or meditate on the past and the hurt that I had suffered. I refused to let the enemy have control of my mind. I was not going to live in self-pity. I was not going to waste my sorrow! I was going to listen to what *God* was saying to me in all of this. I was going to think on things that were true, honest, pure, lovely, and of good report. I was going to saturate my mind with God's Word and His promises.

Have you been betrayed? Have you been violated? Have you been lied about or to? Have you been abandoned? Whatever the hurt, God has a promise for you—peace that passes all understanding is yours when you think and meditate on His Word. The peace of God will keep your heart and mind peaceful, not just by hearing but by putting into practice and obeying God's Word. This is a promise our Father has made to us. We are His children, and He loves us with an everlasting love! (See Jeremiah 31:3; Psalm 136; Isaiah 49:15-16.) I'm not saying that I had total victory all the time. Sometimes I was anxious and troubled. There was quite a battle going on in my mind. There were times I wanted to lash out and make Paul hurt as much as I was hurting. I wanted him to pay for what he had done. I wanted to scream and call names. Forgive? Hah! My emotions at times were up and down. There were times I felt very lonely, angry, troubled, and anxious. However, I knew I couldn't stay in those carnal emotions. I couldn't meditate on the thoughts that were bombarding my mind.

I knew I had joined God's army and there would be battles. During this time in my life, I was in the heat of battle, right there on the front lines. But I refused to go on furlough—rest and relaxation—and just let my mind control me. I was going to pick up my weapon, God's Word, and fight.

I remember flying back from Colorado to Louisiana asking God to give me promises I could stand on during this time of mental combat and conflict. God led me to many promises from His Word and gave so much strength throughout this tough time. His Word is a lamp and a light! The following are a few passages that comforted, strengthened, encouraged, healed, and convicted me during this time of testing:

> *Search me, O God, and know my heart; try me, and know my anxieties; and see if there is any wicked way in me, and lead me in the way everlasting* (Psalm 139:23-24).

> *As for God, His way is perfect; the word of the Lord is proven; He is a shield to all who trust in Him. For who is God, except the Lord? And who is a rock, except our God? It is God who arms me with strength, and makes my way perfect* (Psalm 18:30-32).

As I asked the Lord for a word from His Word, I began to read the psalms, asking God to still my heart and mind. I am so thankful for God speaking to me comfort, strength, healing, forgiveness, assurance, and love.

> *Out of the depths I have cried to You, O Lord; Lord, hear my voice! [Can I tell you that at this time I was definitely in the depths?]*

> *Let Your ears be attentive to the voice of my supplications. If You, Lord, should mark iniquities, [Let's talk about Paul, Lord. Not me!] O Lord, who could stand? But*

there is forgiveness with You, that You may be feared. I wait for the Lord, my soul waits, and in His Word, I do hope. My soul waits for the Lord more than those who watch for the morning—yes, more than those who watch for the morning (Psalm 130:1-6).

As I read these Scriptures, God began to convict my heart. He turned His spotlight on me. As I read verse 3, I was reminded that God doesn't mark our iniquities, He doesn't keep a registry of things we've done wrong. If He did, none of us could stand. Not Paul! Not me! No one! God began to show me what I needed to repent of, what I needed to change. Yes, He did strengthen me and was definitely my Refuge during trouble, but He also showed me areas where I had failed Him.

Did I still have to deal with the unfaithfulness and betrayal? Yes, but I knew I couldn't focus on Paul's sin and ignore my own. I needed to trust God, and not be full of fear, selfishness, anger, anxiety, and any other sin that displeased Him and caused me not to trust Him. Friend, we have a loving Father who forgives and whose love is unconditional.

I quote again from our marriage book. On page 109 I wrote,

> As I gave my mind over to God, every promise I had ever heard, sang in a song, or read in the Bible about God's faithfulness welled up within me. Thoughts that He would never leave me nor forsake me, that He would see me through any and every difficulty, and that He would be my shield and protection against any attack, came to mind as I chose to think about His promises rather than the pain. For every thought of failure and regret and betrayal, God gave me a promise, and in the months to come, Paul and I began to recover and heal.[2]

When I consider the abundance of God's peace, I am reminded of a song we sang years ago called "I've Got Peace Like a River." Every time I think of that first line it fills my heart with such joy and peace, my heart overflows. Oh, how the words still ring true today.

> *I've got peace like a river,*
> *I've got peace like a river,*
> *I've got peace like a river in my soul.*
> *I've got peace like a river,*
> *I've got peace like a river,*
> *I've got peace like a river in my soul.*[3]

In his excellent book on Philippians, *Be Joyful,* Warren Wiersbe wrote:

> The peace of God is one test of whether or not we are in the will of God. *"Let the peace that Christ can give keep on acting as umpire in your hearts"* (Colossians 3:15 WMS). If we are walking with the Lord, then the peace of God and the God of peace exercise their influence over our hearts. Whenever we disobey, we lose that peace, and we know we have done something wrong. God's peace is the "umpire" that calls us out![4]

God's promise of giving peace that passes all of our human understanding is a promise we can stand on. However, we must think on the right things. We must wage war using our spiritual armor to experience His peace. We can't do it in our own strength.

He will keep our hearts *and* minds in and through Christ Jesus. Our hearts and minds aren't kept through reading the Bible, going to church, attending a Bible study, singing, giving, or doing good works. It's through Christ and Christ alone that our hearts and minds are kept peacefully. His Holy Spirit lives in us to empower us to think on the right things. He gives peace that passes all understanding. How? We must choose to think on the right things—*things that are true, honorable, just, pure, lovely, commendable, excellent, and worthy of praise.*

ENDNOTES

1. Author's note: I have excerpted quotes from our book *Get Married, Stay Married*. These quoted excerpts are found on pages 100-106 and 109. You can order this book and any of our ministry resources and materials on our website: www. plowon.org.
2. Ibid.
3. "I've Got Peace Like a River," *Baptist Hymnal* (Nashville, TN: Convention Press, 1975), 458.
4. Warren W. Wiersbe, *Be Joyful* (Wheaton, IL: Victor Books, 1983), 118.

Part II

Entering the Real Field of Battle

God has provided everything you need to successfully stand up to the devil, to resist him, and to defeat him. Will you choose to obey or ignore Paul's urgent command to "put on the whole armor of God?" Your success against an enemy that seeks every opportunity to destroy you depends on the choice you make![1]

Chapter 8

The Well-Dressed Christian

*Do not be anxious about anything, but in everything
by prayer and supplication with thanksgiving let your
requests be made known to God. And the peace of God,
which surpasses all understanding, will guard your
hearts and your minds in Christ Jesus. Finally, brothers,
whatever is true, whatever is honorable, whatever is
just, whatever is pure, whatever is lovely, whatever
is commendable, if there is any excellence, if there is
anything worthy of praise, think about these things.*
—Philippians 4:6-8 ESV

Writing in his daily devotional, "Insight for Today," Charles Swindoll shared a quote from *Happiness Is a Choice*, written by two Christian physicians, Frank Minirth and Paul Meier:

> As psychiatrists, we cringe whenever Christian patients use the word "can't." Any good psychiatrist knows that "I can't" and "I've tried" are merely lame excuses. We insist that our patients be honest with themselves and use language that expresses

the reality of the situation. So, we have our patients change their can'ts to won'ts. If some individual changes all their can'ts to won'ts, they stop avoiding the truth, quit deceiving themselves and start living in reality.[2]

THE FULL ARMOR OF GOD

I've encouraged many women to read Joyce Meyer's book *Battlefield of the Mind.* When I see them again, I ask if they've read it. "Yes," they reply. I then ask, "Have you put into practice what it says in the book?" Their answer usually is, "Well, it's so hard!" Yes, it is hard, but it's the way to have victory over the enemy. Satan loves to discourage, defeat, and destroy God's children. Our mind is the battlefield. We must put on the *whole armor* of God to defeat this enemy.

In Ephesians 6, the apostle Paul gave us the armor to put on to have victory over the enemy. He painted a beautiful picture of what the "well-dressed Christian" should look like. He wrote:

> *Finally, be strong in the Lord and in his mighty power. Put on the full armor of God, so that you can take your stand against the devil's schemes. For our struggle is not against flesh and blood, but against the rulers, against the authorities, against the powers of this dark world and against the spiritual forces of evil in the heavenly realms. Therefore put on the full armor of God, so that when the day of evil comes, you may be able to stand your ground, and after you have done everything, to stand. Stand firm then, with the belt of truth buckled around your waist, with the breastplate of righteousness in place, and with your feet fitted with the readiness that comes from the*

*gospel of peace. In addition to all this, take up the shield
of faith, with which you can extinguish all the flaming
arrows of the evil one. Take the helmet of salvation and
the sword of the Spirit, which is the word of God. And
pray in the Spirit on all occasions with all kinds of prayers
and requests. With this in mind, be alert and always keep
on praying for all the Lord's people* (Ephesians 6:10-18
NIV).

A well-dressed Christian will put on:

Belt of Truth: Satan is the father of lies. Truth is truth,
which is the Word of God. The idea of absolute truth is insep-
arable from the life of Jesus Christ and from the Bible. In
John 14:6, Jesus defined Himself as *"the way, the truth, and the
life"* He also defined the Word of God as truth: *"Sanctify them by
Your truth. Your word is truth"* (John 17:17). As far as the world
is concerned, there are no absolutes. But God's Word is the
anchor—Jesus Christ and the Bible, the Word of God, represent absolute truth! You've probably heard it said, "God said it!
I believe it! That settles it!" No! Rather, God said it! And that
settles it, whether we believe it or not!

O.S. Hawkins shared the following about the danger
of relativism:

> We in the Western world have raised a couple of gen-
> erations who have few, if any, absolutes. Relativism
> guides their thought processes, so it is increasingly
> difficult to convince them than sin exists. Consider
> sex as an example. It is God's beautiful and special
> gift to us. However, used wrongly, sex has a destruc-
> tive and often debilitating effect on those involved.
> Most people don't realize that sexual sin is different
> from all other sin. It is the sole sin a person commits

not only against God but against himself or herself as well (1 Corinthians 6:18). Furthermore, our bodies are the temple, the dwelling place, of the Holy Spirit (v. 19). In the Old Covenant times, God had a temple for His people. But, in our dispensation of grace, God has a people for His temple. You—your very body—is His dwelling place. Do not be deceived about sin. Keep pure for Him.[3]

Breastplate of Righteousness: Christ is our righteousness. He protects our hearts. Adam Clarke's Commentary says the following: "As the breast-plate defends the heart and lungs, and all those vital functionaries that are contained in what is called the region of the thorax; so, this righteousness defends everything on which the man's spiritual existence depends."[4]

Feet shod with the gospel of peace: We must be prepared and ready when battles come our way. The gospel itself is to be the firm footing of believers, our walk being worthy of it and therefore a testimony in regard to it.

Shield of Faith: We can be sure that our Father will keep His promises, even when we doubt. Faith is an unshakable belief in the promises of God.

Helmet of Salvation: We must believe that Jesus Christ is God and trust Him for our life. We must believe that He died and rose again for us: *"But God demonstrates His own love toward us, in that while we were still sinners, Christ died for us. Much more then, having now been justified by His blood, we shall be saved from wrath through Him. For if when we were enemies we were reconciled to God through the death of His Son, much more, having been reconciled, we shall be saved by His life"* (Romans 5:8-10).

The Sword of the Spirit: "...*and the sword of the Spirit, which is the word of God*" (Ephesians 6:17). The sword of the Spirit is the only weapon of offense in the armor, but the Word, the Bible, is also a tool for defense. God's Word has the power to change how we think. It can change the way we feel, the way we live, and the way we love.

I love what Mark Batterson wrote in his book *Whisper* about the power of God's Word:

> The Word of God is longer than the longest memory and stronger than the strongest imagination. It's also deeper than the cortex of the brain.[5]

But, we must do what the psalmist himself did: *"Your word I have hidden in my heart, that I might not sin against You"* (Psalm 119:11). There arc people with dementia or brain damage who don't know their spouse or children, yet when a hymn is sung, they begin to sing along. They can quote Scripture, God's truth, yet they have little sense of their physical surroundings. A person whose spirit has been quickened by God's Spirit is powerful.

> *For the word of God is living and powerful, and sharper than any two-edged sword, piercing even to the division of soul and spirit, and of joints and marrow, and is a discerner of the thoughts and intents of the heart* (Hebrews 4:12).

POSITIVE SELF-TALK

Paul and I took our children—Mark, Gretchen, Paul Edward, Melanie, Thom, and Kelley—to New York City for a few days. While there we toured many places, including the 9/11 Memorial. On our way to tour the memorial, we talked about where we were during that horrific incident. Paul and I were in Skiatook, Oklahoma, when it occurred. I can remember the fear and anxiety that enveloped me when I saw this atrocity being televised. I wanted to gather all of my children and grandchildren together and take them to a safe place. I wrote of my sadness and fear in a journal, and as I looked back in my journal, I realized it took me a few days to get over my fear. It's amazing how fear can take hold of us and not let go. However, I knew I had to trust God and start talking to myself instead of listening to myself.

In Chapter 2, "Why Worry When You Can Rest?" I shared about speaking to ourselves in psalms, hymns, and spiritual songs. Our minds are constantly thinking on something. A thought is not a sin, but we can allow our minds to control us when thoughts that are not godly enter our thinking process. When our thoughts are honoring to our Lord and His Word, we think on things that are pure, honest, lovely, just, and commendable. If our thoughts are *not* pleasing to the Lord, immediately snatch that thought out and get rid of it before that seed becomes a deep-rooted oak tree.

Throughout our marriage, I had to stand on God's Word and know that He had everything under control. We women, who are emotional creatures, have a tendency to allow our emotions to control us. Yes, emotions are necessary at times, and God uses our emotions—but they shouldn't control us. They shouldn't be our masters, but our servants. We need to remember that God is not taken by surprise by anything that happens in the world. He knows everything; therefore, we can trust and depend on Him. I can rest in His promises. There's no "Oops" in His vocabulary.

When we lived in Louisiana in the 1970s and '80s, Paul was gone quite a bit. Actually, he was gone a lot, so I pretty much raised our children. Even though I had a wonderful church family, there were days I would get lonely. When the children were in school, I would sit in the front yard and wonder if Paul was going to come home. What would I do if something happened to him? I would allow my mind to take me to a place that seemed hopeless. We had an old piano and when I wasn't in the front yard, I would sit and play and sing. I wasn't a good pianist, but I could play chords, so I would make up songs using God's Word. Using Scriptures to make up songs would encourage my heart and focus my mind on the right things. As I sang, my anxiety would dissipate. During times like these, God's Word was a soothing balm. It was powerful!

I remember one particular time when I was so defeated and just felt dead inside. I would read God's Word, but it had no meaning. I prayed, but it seemed, to no avail. When Paul would call, I would tell him how I felt. He encouraged me to read the psalms on praise. I did that, but it didn't seem to help. I remember sitting down one day and writing how worthless I was, how ugly I was, how defeated I was, what a terrible wife and mother I was, and on and on.

However, every time I picked up a book or the Bible, I would read the passage of Scripture where it talked about Jesus praying for me—ever interceding for me. I believe this is what brought me out of my deadness, my self-pity, anxiety or whatever it was I was living in. I knew if no one else was praying for me, Jesus was and is. *"He always lives to make intercession for them* [His children]" (Hebrews 7:25). Stop and think about this! Jesus is at the right hand of the Father, and He's praying for you. What a great promise to hold on to in every situation of life. We can count on Him. Don't give up! Keep on keeping on! *Plow on! Plow on! Plow on!* James MacDonald said:

> Doubt is a lack of confidence or assurance that God will keep His promises. Doubt is the mind-set that keeps saying, "Well, I just don't know if God will keep His promises…." Doubt involves a settled and persistent choice to live with uncertainty. It's not the stubborn "show me" of Thomas, that went looking

for answers, but the steady unresolved attitude of Jonah that said, in effect, "I don't know and I don't care. I don't believe and nobody can change that." Such doubt is dangerous. It's destructive and completely detrimental to any kind of relationship with God. I mean, if you don't have confidence that God will keep His promises, what do you have?[6]

Let me encourage you to find your own promises. I have a book titled *Promises from God's Word* that I've had since 1982. I've turned to this promise book many times through the years when I was anxious about something. Why not make your own promise book and mark down the promises God gives you as He speaks to your heart, and mark the dates when He answers those promises. As you look back through the years, you will be encouraged as you review all the times God has answered your prayers as you stood on His promises. This will grow your faith!

YOUR THOUGHT LIFE

How would you describe your thought life? Once you describe it, where do the thoughts come from? Yes, from our heart. I'm not talking about thoughts that just pop into our head all day long and then are gone. I'm talking about those thoughts that we decide to meditate on. Those thoughts that are displeasing to the Lord and destructive to our lives. It's when we decide to make them part of our lives and meditate on them that they become sin.

We must understand that something drives our thoughts! We have a nature, a heart condition that actively influences our thought life. The desires inside our hearts lure and entice us. Out of our hearts, thoughts flow! And because we have a heart condition that is either very, very sick or being healed by our Savior, we must take seriously the state of our hearts. Check it out!

> *Those who are dominated by the sinful nature think about sinful things, but those who are controlled by the Holy Spirit think about things that please the Spirit* (Romans 8:5 New Living Translation).

> *For from the heart come evil thoughts...* (Matthew 15:19 New Living Translation).

Out of our hearts come the thoughts that we think! Our hearts are full of all kinds of desires, and our desires are often expressed via our thoughts. While intricately connected, we must understand that the condition of our heart directly impacts the nature of our thought life. If we are dominated by our sinful nature and heart, then our thoughts will set out to destroy us and all God loves. If we are controlled by the Holy Spirit of God, our thoughts will bring life and joy to our existence and even to the lives of those around us![7]

So, in order to think right, we must have a new heart: "*And I will give you a new heart, and I will put a new spirit in you. I will take out your stony, stubborn heart and give you a tender, responsive heart*" (Ezekiel 36:26 New Living Translation). Ezekiel declared that God is the One who gives us a new heart and puts a new spirit in us. It is God who transforms us and changes the way we think.

God's Holy Spirit, who lives within us, will give us the power to think on the things that are right. But we must know what's right in order to think on what's pleasing to God. God's Word is true, so when we know His Word, we can run everything by this grid: Does this thought glorify God? Is what I'm thinking pleasing to my heavenly Father? Trying to use self-control won't work. Or, sitting in a prone position with our fingers in a circle and humming while mediating won't do the trick either. If we could do it ourselves, we wouldn't need Jesus. Apart from Jesus, we can do nothing!

Whatever is true: Truth! Jesus said, *"I am the way, the truth, and the life. No man comes to the Father except through Me"* (John 14:6).

Whatever is honorable: The word "honorable" means honest. Are you thinking on things that are honorable? Is this thought honoring God? Is it honoring your husband? Is it honoring your children?

Whatever is just: Innocent, holy, or righteous! Can you write "holy" over your thoughts?

Whatever is pure: Innocent! Chaste! Clean! Modest!

Whatever is lovely: Acceptable. Acceptable to whom? To our heavenly Father. To our husband. To our children.

Whatever is commendable: That which is well spoken of or reputable. Are your thoughts reputable? Would they be well spoken of by others if they were spoken out loud? Good question!

My dear friend, if there is any virtue, excellence, or anything worthy of praise, we must think on these things—the right things.

Verse 9 in Philippians 4 tells us that when we think on the things that are pleasing to God, He will be with us. His peace will be with us. This is a great promise. Apostle Paul is speaking to Christians and encouraging them to practice what he has taught them, and what he has lived before them: *"The things which you learned and received and heard and saw in me, these do, and the God of peace will be with you"* (Philippians 4:9).

ENDNOTES

1. Rick Renner, *Sparkling Gems from the Greek* (Tulsa, OK: Teach All Nations), 321.

2. Charles R. Swindoll, "Insight for Today—Can't…or Won't? Part Two"; www.insight.org/resources/daily-devotional/individual/can't-.-.-.-or-won't-part-two; accessed August 1, 2018.

3. O.S. Hawkins, *The James Code* (Nashville, TN: Thomas Nelson, 2015), 56.

4. Adam Clarke, *Bible Commentary in 8 Volumes: Volume 7, Epistle of Paul the Apostle to the Ephesians* (New York: Scriptura Press, 2015), 40.

5. Mark Batterson, *Whisper: How to Hear the Voice of God* (Colorado Springs, CO: Multnomah, 2017).

6. James MacDonald, *Lord, Change My Attitude: Before It's Too Late* (Chicago, IL. Moody Publishers, 2001), 139-140.

7. Susan Thomas, "Is My Problem My Thought Life?" *Association of Biblical Counselors* (blog), August 11, 2011, https://christiancounseling.com/blog/uncategorized/is-my-problem-my-thought-life/; accessed August 9, 2018.

Part III

Tackling the Tongue

THE TONGUE

Its power is mighty
To bless or to curse.
It can make you feel better,
It can make you feel worse.
It's compared to a serpent,
a viper, a snake.
I have total control
Unless I'm awake.
Though it's small as a bit
Or a ship's tiny rudder,
The words it can say
Can make your heart shudder.
Gossip and nagging,
Praises and hymns,
How can this thing
Do all on a whim?
Be wise in the way
You speak to others;
Remember in Christ,
They're our sisters and brothers.
Let the light of Christ
Show on your face.
Let your words be seasoned
with love and grace.

Thru Christ you have power
whether written or sung.
Take hold of the bridle
or be hung by the tongue!
—Lisa Simmons

Chapter 9

Out of the Same Mouth

With the tongue we praise our Lord and Father, and with it we curse human beings, who have been made in God's likeness. Out of the same mouth come praise and cursing. My brothers and sisters, this should not be.
—James 3:9-10 NIV

THE APOSTLE PAUL, LIKE JAMES, UNDERSTOOD THE IMPORtance of encouraging others with our words. He said, *"Do not let any unwholesome talk come out of your mouths, but only what is helpful for building others up according to their needs, that it may benefit those who listen"* (Ephesians 4:29 NIV).

In other words, we must avoid using words that discourage. Our aim should be to use words that will encourage and bring hope to a person. To encourage means to cheer, motivate, spur on, embolden, fortify, and invigorate. Jesus said, *"...the mouth speaks what the heart is full of"* (Matthew 12:34 NIV). If our words don't meet God's standard, don't say them. And, just because something is in our brain does not mean it should come out of our mouth! Just obey God's Word.

The tongue truly is the showcase of the heart! Whatever is going on in the heart is what comes flowing from our mouths. When we are filled with the Holy Spirit of God, that is the first manifestation that will come out of our mouths—through our tongues and our lips. Instead of murmuring, complaining, criticizing, and giving vent to unbelief, the apostle Paul said we should speak, sing, make music, and give thanks to the Lord. The entire use of our tongues will be positive, not negative.

Proverbs 18:21 (NIV) says, *"The tongue has the power of life and death, and those who love it will eat its fruit."* You can see the seriousness of our words—our words kill or they give life; they are either poison or sweet-tasting fruit. The choice is up to you! Words have killed or damaged, marriages, friendships, careers, families, etc. I don't know about you, but I want to choose good words because I never know when I'm going to need someone to encourage me, comfort me, speak blessings over me, help restore me, and grant me forgiveness. I want to show kindness because that's what I would want someone to show me.

I'm sure you've heard the great command to "Do unto others as you would have them do to you." It's *not* do unto others as they do to you. Let's get this right! A verse I've quoted to myself many, many times throughout my years is *"Post a guard at my mouth, God, set a watch at the door of my lips"* (Psalm 141:3 The Message). This verse helps me when I want to lash back at Paul or say things to a friend that don't need to be said. I have a plaque in front of my sink in the kitchen to remind of this very thing. It says, *"Lord, keep Your arm around my shoulder and Your hand over my mouth."*

> *A careless word may kindle strife,*
> *a cruel word may wreck a life,*
> *a timely word may lessen stress,*
> *a loving word may heal and bless.*
> —Author unknown

I was reading a book the other day and I found this profound statement: "Blessed is the woman who, having nothing to say, abstains from giving us wordy evidence of the fact."

This little member called the tongue has the power to bless or curse, encourage or discourage. I remind you that James said, *"Out of the same mouth come praise and cursing. My brothers and sisters, this should not be."* Let me share with you some of the positive and negative words this little weapon can use for better or worse.

A Tongue that Lies

A Negative Tongue (exaggerates):

> *Deliver my soul, O Lord, from lying lips and from a deceitful tongue* (Psalm 120:2).

This should be our prayer every day. How easy is it to say, "It's just a little white lie?" No, my friend, there are no little white lies—just lies. Lying is mentioned twice when God states the seven things He hates: *"These six things the Lord hates, yes, seven are an abomination to Him: …a lying tongue… a false witness who breathes out lies"* (Proverbs 6:16-19 ESV). Because He says this twice in this Scripture passage, I believe it's a serious offense.

When our children were very young, Paul Edward, our middle child, had a terrible habit of lying. When the truth would be better, he still lied. There's a Scripture I made him memorize and quote every time he lied, *"Lying lips are an abomination to the Lord…"* (Proverbs 12:22). I must say that he is now one of the most truthful young men I know; of course, I may be a little prejudice! However, I never made him learn the rest of the verse. I just focused on the negative and not the positive part of this promise. The rest of the verse says, *"…but those who deal truthfully are His delight"* (Proverbs 12:22). I believe we have to emphasize the positive in order to alleviate the negative. Truth must replace a lie!

A Positive Tongue

Jesus prayed, *"Sanctify them* [His disciples and all who would believe in Him] *by Your truth. Your word is truth"* (John 17:17).

> *Therefore each of you must put off all falsehood* [lying] *and speak truthfully to your neighbor, for we are all members of one body* (Ephesians 4:25 NIV).

> *My son, do not forget my law, but let your heart keep my commands; for length of days and long life and peace they will add to you. Let not mercy and truth forsake you; bind them around your neck, write them on the tablet of your heart, and so find favor and high esteem in the sight of God and man* (Proverbs 3:1-4).

Jesus says in John 14:6 that He is the one and only way, the truth, and He is life! No one comes to the Father but by Him. If you want to know "truth," you need to know Jesus.

How many times have we heard the saying, beauty is only skin deep? This is so true. For instance, I've seen women who are stunningly beautiful, but the moment they open their mouth and began to talk, the beauty turns to ugliness. I've seen very plain and somewhat homely women who became beautiful right before my eyes as they began to use gracious and lovely words as they spoke.

A Tongue that Boasts

A Negative Tongue

> *For who makes you differ from another? And what do you have that you did not receive? Now if you did indeed*

receive it, why do you boast as if you had not received it?
(1 Corinthians 4:7).

This Scripture makes me think of an Old Testament king by the name of Nebuchadnezzar. We read in the Book of Daniel how he boasted about the beautiful city he built by his own mighty power to serve as his royal residence and as an expression of his royal splendor. Daniel 4:31 says *"While the word was still in the king's mouth, a voice fell from heaven: 'King Nebuchadnezzar, to you it is spoken: the kingdom has departed from you!'"*

The king was driven from his palace and lived like a derelict with hair that grew like feathers of an eagle and his nails like the claws of a bird. He ate grass like an ox. He was driven from among the people. He became mentally ill. He lived like this for seven years. At the end of that time, he raised his eyes toward Heaven, and his sanity was restored. He praised God and honored and glorified Him who lives forever.

I think we can take a lesson from Nebuchadnezzar. Even though the king was warned in a dream that these things would come to pass (Daniel interpreted the dream—see Daniel 4:24-33), he refused to believe this could happen to him. I'm sure the king thought there was no way in the world he could go from being the most powerful king in the known world to living like an animal. Proverbs 27:1 says, *"Do not boast about tomorrow, for you do not know what a day may bring forth."* We must remember that every talent, ability, or possession we have, and all the praise and accolades we receive, come from the Lord.

A Positive Tongue

Let another man praise you, and not your own mouth; a stranger, and not your own lips (Proverbs 27:2).

*Humble yourselves in the sight of the Lord, and He will
lift you up* (James 4:10).

I believe if we don't humble ourselves, God has His ways of
humbling us. How do I know? I've been there! But I must say,
His ways, although hard, are necessary.

A Tongue that Slanders

A Negative Tongue

Whoever goes about slandering reveals secrets...
(Proverbs 11:13 ESV).

I was curious about the definition of slander, so I looked in
the dictionary and found it is used as a noun and a verb.

Noun: Character assassination; malicious gossip.
These are just a few of the words used to describe
how someone can slander another person. Verb: to
blacken someone's name; to tell lies about; or speak
ill/evil of; to sully someone's reputation; smear; cast
aspersions on; spread scandal about. I'm sure you get
the picture. When I hear someone doing this to a
person, it doesn't make me think badly of the one
talked about, but the one who was doing the talking.
Just saying!

A Positive Tongue

...but he who is trustworthy in spirit keeps a thing covered
(Proverbs 11:13 ESV).

*Set a guard over my mouth, Lord; keep watch over the
door of my lips* (Psalm 141:3 NIV).

I can't tell you how many times I have quoted this Scripture.
It's a present help in time of need. We must remember that

God's Word is the greatest weapon we have in our Christian arsenal. Let's use it!

A Tongue that Manipulates

A Negative Tongue

A dialogue between Samson and Delilah: "She said, 'How can you say 'I love you' when you don't even trust me? Three times now you've toyed with me, like a cat with a mouse, refusing to tell me the secret of your great strength." She kept at it day after day, nagging and tormenting him. Finally, he was fed up—he couldn't take another minute of it. He spilled the secret (see Judges 16:15-17). I can just see Delilah sitting there with Samson's head in her lap, twisting his long hair, her lower lip curled in a pout, eyes looking as though she is hurt.

I believe we can all identify with this tactic to some extent. However, we need to know that this type of getting our way is not pleasing to the Lord. This is a crafty use of our tongue to get what we want: "If you loved me you would buy this for me. If you really cared, you would do this for me." In other words, if you don't give into my whining and nagging and letting me get my way, you prove you don't really love me. How foolish can we be when we think like this! We don't want to be like Delilah.

My dear friend, trust God with what you desire. He will meet every need of your heart. I didn't say He would meet every want but every *need*.

A Positive Tongue

> *She opens her mouth with wisdom, and on her tongue is the law of kindness.... Charm is deceitful and beauty is passing* [vain], *but a woman who fears the Lord, she shall be praised* (Proverbs 31:26,30).

A TONGUE THAT GOSSIPS

A Negative Tongue

> *Rumors are dainty morsels that sink deep into one's heart*
> (Proverbs 18:8 New Living Translation).

A person who gossips may tell things about someone they know or someone they don't know. They may say to someone, "I heard so and so about this person, but I wasn't sure it was true. Have you heard anything?" This gossip is looking for information. Don't partake of this sin. Simply say, "I haven't heard anything," even if you have heard something. "Let's pray right now for that situation." Then, why not take the person's hand and pray for the person being gossiped about. Many of us have been in prayer meetings when someone wanted to pray for a person, and then they proceed to tell all the details of the person's life, or they say, "I really shouldn't say this, but …!" If you know you shouldn't say it, *don't!*

Gossip hurts the one who is listening, the one spoken about, and the conscience of the one telling it. Also, those of us who are willing to listen are just as guilty of gossip. There have been so many times I've been around someone talking negatively about a person. I am tempted to put in my two cents worth rather than stop the conversation by saying something good and turning the conversation to a positive note. Oh, I have been guilty of joining in the negative talk, but my spirit is grieved every time I do it. I have to continually remind myself that I wouldn't want someone talking negatively about me—do unto others as you want them to do to you.

When I taught a young married women's class many years ago, I had a pastor friend draw a picture for me. I told him I wanted a picture of a giant ear with a large trashcan above the ear. I wanted trash to be pouring into the ear. Nothing had to be written on the picture. We all understood it's meaning.

Don't partake or listen to someone who is maligning another person. Remember, if they are gossiping about someone to you, they will gossip about you.

I love this quote by William Hazlitt: "To create an unfavourable impression, it is not necessary that certain things should be true, but that they have been said."[1]

When Paul and I lived in Louisiana, there were many wonderful people who came from all over to attend Bible conferences four times a year. This was such an exciting time for us as a family. Our children looked forward to it as much as Paul and I did. They could hardly wait for school to be out so they could go to the conference grounds and help everyone get settled in their rooms for the week. I, along with the children, would prepare food for forty to fifty people every night after the conference, and we would sit and fellowship in our home until we couldn't keep our eyes open. It was a glorious time.

However, there were many times a couple would bring news, or gossip, about other people, demeaning their character. We may not have known them, or even knew if the tales were true, but we certainly believed and repeated the news. I write this with great shame for this season in our lives, but I share this now to encourage anyone who is practicing this to remember God's promise—we reap what we sow! Paul and I certainly did, and it almost devastated our family.

How true God's Word is when it says we reap what we sow (see Galatians 6:7). It may not be today or tomorrow, but reaping will come. The way we love, we will be loved. The way we forgive, we will be forgiven. The way we give, it will be given to us. Whether it be positive or negative, we will reap what we sow.

Let me encourage you to memorize this Scripture: *"Do not let any unwholesome talk come out of your mouths, but only what is helpful for building others up according to their needs that it may benefit those who listen"* (Ephesians 4:29 NIV). As I have already mentioned, but it is worth repeating, unless what you say encourages, uplifts, ministers grace and edifies a person, *don't say it!* Let's keep our mouths shut! When someone says, "I really shouldn't tell you this, but...." We need to say, "Then I don't want to hear it."

A Positive Tongue

> *When there are many words, transgression and offense are unavoidable, but he who controls his lips and keeps thoughtful silence is wise* (Proverbs 10:19 Amplified Bible).

> *For lack of wood the fire goes out, and where there is no whisperer [who gossips], contention quiets down* (Proverbs 26:20 Amplified Bible).

> *Let my lips speak praise [with thanksgiving], for You teach me Your statutes. Let my tongue sing [praise for the fulfillment] of Your word for all Your commandments are righteous* (Psalm 119:171-172 Amplified Bible).

> *Understand this, my beloved brothers and sisters. Let everyone be quick to hear [be a careful, thoughtful listener], slow to speak [a speaker of carefully chosen words and], slow to anger [patient, reflective, forgiving]* (James 1:19 Amplified Bible).

> A word of encouragement during a failure is worth more than an hour of praise after success (Author unknown).

A Tongue that Betrays

A Negative Tongue

> *A gossip betrays a confidence* [discloses, divulges, tells, gives away, leaks, unmasks, exposes]... (Proverbs 11:13 NIV).

I remember Paul telling me about a management team meeting he was in when the leader told the members that what was being said that day was confidential. One member raised his hand and said, "I don't have a problem with keeping a confidence. It's the one I tell who has the problem." Everyone laughed because he was joking. However, when a friend confides in us, it's grievous to violate this trust. When I hear someone say, "Now, this is confidential," I know they can't keep a secret. A betrayer is usually talking about a friend. A gossiper is talking about anyone convenient.

One of my all-time favorite devotionals was given to me in 1987—*Come Before Winter and Share My Hope* by Charles Swindoll. One of the powerful devotions is titled "Keeping Confidences." I'm going to quote him because I can't state it better than he did:

> Information is powerful. The person who receives it and dispenses it bit by bit often does so that others may be impressed because he or she is "in the know." Few things are more satisfying to the old ego than having others stare wide-eyed, drop open the jaw, and say, "My, I didn't know that!" or "Wow, that's hard to believe!" or "How in the world did you find that out?"[2]

Pastor Swindoll also quoted some of the wise sayings of Solomon in the Proverbs (New American Standard Bible):

Wise men store up knowledge, but with the mouth of the foolish, ruin is at hand (10:14).

He who goes about as a talebearer reveals secrets, but he who is trustworthy conceals a matter (11:13).

The one who guards his mouth preserves his life; the one who opens wide his lips comes to ruin (13:3).

Like a bad tooth and an unsteady foot is confidence in a faithless man in time of trouble (25:19).

A Positive Tongue

But he who is of a faithful spirit conceals a matter (Proverbs 11:13).

When a friend asks you to keep a secret, the person is trusting you to not betray him or her by telling someone else. If the person agrees you can share with your spouse, the person is trusting the spouse not to tell anyone.

In the same article, Charles Swindoll reveals four practical ground rules we should establish in our lives:

Whatever you're told in confidence, *do not repeat.*

Whenever you're tempted to talk, *do not yield.*

Whenever you're discussing people, *do not gossip.*

However you're prone to disagree, *do not slander.*[3]

A TONGUE THAT COMPLAINS AND MURMURS

A Negative Tongue

How long shall I bear with this evil congregation, that murmur [complain] against me? I have heard the murmurings of the children of Israel, which they murmur against me (Numbers 14:27 American Standard Version).

I spoke to a group of ladies in California a few years ago, and my subject was tackling the tongue. I wanted to talk about getting this dangerous weapon we have in our mouths under control. I was curious about the subject of complaining and murmuring, so I researched "complaining" on the Internet. I couldn't believe the number of websites I found.

There are actually websites to go to for the express purpose of: complaining, letting off steam, whining, venting your anger, and however else you want to sound off about what is upsetting you. You can receive feedback from others who are venting their frustrations as well. All of this is for the world to see, or should I say read. You can even post your name and a picture. Really? Why would anyone want to share their baggage with people who can't help their situation, or share with those who really don't care?

As mentioned previously in this book, complaining and murmuring got the children of Israel in big trouble. They thought they were murmuring against Moses, but in Numbers 14:27 we see they were murmuring against God! He's the One who: delivered them from bondage, parted the Red Sea, fed them while in the wilderness; clothed them, provided water when they needed it, and, kept Pharaoh's army from catching up to them.

Yet, they complained and murmured, which led to disobedience. They saw miracle after miracle, yet they complained! I don't know about you, but I am so blessed that I would be an ungrateful daughter to complain or murmur about anything. After all, God says He works everything for our good and His glory. He also says in First Thessalonians 5:18 that we are to give thanks for everything, for this is His will for us. Do we understand everything? No, but we can trust our Father.

A Positive Tongue

Do all things without complaining and disputing, that you may become blameless and harmless, children of God without fault in the midst of a crooked and perverse generation, among whom you shine as lights in the world (Philippians 2:14-15).

And whatever you do in word or deed, do all in the name of the Lord Jesus, giving thanks to God the Father through Him (Colossians 3:17).

When we have a grateful heart, I believe we will find it hard to complain and murmur.

ENDNOTES

1. William Hazlitt, *Characteristics* (1823); https://en.wikiquote.org/wiki/William_Hazlitt; accessed August 19, 2018.
2. Charles R. Swindoll, "Insight for Today—Keeping Confidences"; https://www.insight.org/resources/daily-devotional/individual/keeping-confidences; accessed August 19, 2018.
3. Ibid.

Chapter 10

Out of the Same Mouth, Continued

*So also the tongue is a small member, yet it boasts
of great things. How great a forest is set ablaze by
such a small fire! And the tongue is a fire, a world
of unrighteousness. The tongue is set among our
members, staining the whole body, setting on fire
the entire course of life, and set on fire by hell.*
—James 3:5-6 ESV

As WE CONTINUE TO LOOK AT THE NEGATIVE AND POSITIVE
aspects of the tongue, I am reminded of something I read
many years ago. In his book *James Your Brother,* Lehman
Strauss wrote:

> Mountain climbers have said that there are certain
> times and places when the vibration from a faint
> whisper could bring down an avalanche. Whenever
> the guide detects such sensitivity in the air, he cau-
> tions every climber to remain silent. Our Lord said,

"Not that which goeth into the mouth defileth a man; but that which cometh out of the mouth, this defileth a man (Matthew 15:11). Oh, let us not be guilty of sinning with the tongue.[1]

Now, let's continue.

A TONGUE THAT CURSES

A Negative Tongue

From the same mouth come blessing and cursing. My brothers, these things ought not to be so (James 3:10 ESV).

I don't believe this verse is talking about what we call "swear words," even though it could be because everything we say should be to edify and uplift and should glorify God. The word "curse" means disgusting, disgraceful, hateful, or vile. I believe when we speak evil about a person—when we malign their character, tell them they are mean, ugly, wicked, stupid, dumb, never amount to anything, and the list could go on— this is cursing them, not blessing them.

I have heard mothers say to (and about) their children: "He's so stubborn! He's so mean! He won't listen! She won't obey. She's so bossy! She has a mind of her own!" It's as though they are bragging about their child's misbehavior rather than being grieved over it. Remember, our children will live up to what we say!

I remember one particular server at a restaurant in Louisiana. She was very friendly, so we began to talk to her. She started telling us about her son. The first words out of her mouth were, "He's so mean." This is called a curse. Without realizing it, she was speaking a curse over her son. I said to her, "Your son will live up to what you say about him. You need to bless him; tell him what a great son he is, how smart he is, how polite he is, how respectful he is. He will live up to your expectations." Whether we believe it or not, our children want to please us from the time they are born. If we say they are obedient, they want to live up to that. If we say they are stubborn and self-willed, they will live up to that.

When I wrote my book *Operation Blessing*, this is what I was doing for my children and grandchildren. I was speaking blessings over their lives. I want them to know that God has a wonderful plan for their lives. He wants to bless them with a life that is abundant.

> *Now to Him who is able to do exceedingly abundantly above all that we ask or think, according to the power that works in us* (Ephesians 3:20).

I know a friend who has carried a piece of paper around with him for many years. On the paper is a note from his father who told him he would never amount to anything. He said a few other hurtful things that caused deep wounds in his son's heart. This son believes what his father wrote on this piece of paper, so his life has been very difficult. Rather than throw that paper away and believe God's Word, he has lived out his father's curse.

A Positive Tongue

> *Now may the God of peace Himself sanctify you completely; and may your whole spirit, soul, and body be preserved blameless at the coming of our Lord Jesus Christ. He who calls you is faithful, who also will do it* (1 Thessalonians 5:23-24).

These verses constitute a blessing the apostle Paul spoke to the church at Thessalonica. Paul reminded them that they are saints, and he could see Christ in their lives. He starts out his letters to the churches or individuals by speaking well of them and letting them know how proud he is of them. He wants them to know how thankful he is for their friendship. Why don't we start each day speaking blessings on our family?

I heard a pastor talk about a man who was constantly complaining about his work. He would say things like "This damn business." Well, that's what he was doing to his business. He was speaking curses on it. Our words have power. We can speak blessings or curses on our business, family, or friends.

> *Death and life are in the power of the tongue, and those who love it and indulge it will eat its fruit and bear the consequences of their words* (Proverbs 18:21 Amplified Bible).

> *Pleasant words are like a honeycomb, sweet and delightful to the soul and healing to the body* (Proverbs 16:24 Amplified Bible).

A TONGUE THAT JUDGES

A Negative Tongue

> *Judge not, that you be not judged. For with the judgment you pronounce you will be judged, and with the measure you use it will be measured to you. Why do you see the speck that is in your brother's eye, but do not notice the log that is in your own eye? Or how can you say to your brother, "Let me take the speck out of your eye," when there is the log in your own eye? You hypocrite, first take the log out of your own eye, and then you will see clearly to take the speck out of your brother's eye* (Matthew 7:1-5 ESV).

Strong's Concordance notes that the word translated "judge" in Matthew 7:1 can also mean condemn. What Christ is saying is that we are incapable of seeing a person's heart or knowing his or her relationship with God. We are not to take the place of God in making judgments about someone's motives or eternal salvation. And we should be humble, knowing our own weaknesses and sins.

> God does not take kindly our attempts to sit on His Throne and act like we are Him in trying to change or fix others. We are the servants and He is the Lord. We are helpers not the Holy Spirit (Wade Trimmer).

It saddens me to say that I was so judgmental and legalistic in my early years as a Christian. However, God did a great work of grace in my heart in the 1980s. I have found that once God humbles us, we tend to have more grace. We aren't so quick to cast aspersions on others. We have a softer, more forgiving heart.

A Positive Tongue

The following is from an article from Bible.org titled "What is the difference between discernment and being judgmental?"

> It is important to understand the difference between being judgmental, and discerning truth from error. In Matt. 7:1, the Lord said, *"Do not judge lest you be judged."* Then, in verses 2-5 he warns against trying to correct others without first correcting what is wrong in our own lives. If we deal honestly with our own hearts, etc., then we have the responsibility to help others. But there is also a warning in verse 6. He said, *"Do not give what is holy to dogs, and do not throw your pearls before swine"* (vs. 6).

How can we know that someone, in their spiritual condition, is like a dog or a pig (i.e., someone who is incapable of appreciating the truth—apathetic, cold, indifferent), unless you judge, discern their character or their spiritual condition?

This passage does not teach that judgments should never be made. In fact, *Matthew 7:5* specifically speaks of removing the speck from your brother's eye. But the Lord's point is that no one is qualified nor able to do that if they are habitually critical or condemnatory of the specks in someone else's eye when they themselves have a plank—a hyperbole for effect—in their own eye. Such are not truly interested in righteousness, only in playing spiritual king of the mountain.[2]

Judge not, and you will not be judged; condemn not, and you will not be condemned; forgive, and you will be forgiven; give, and it will be given to you. Good measure, pressed down, shaken together, running over, will be put into your lap. For with the measure you use it will be measured back to you (Luke 6:37-38 ESV).

You do well when you complete the Royal Rule of the Scriptures: "Love others as you love yourself. …Talk and act like a person expecting to be judged by the Rule that sets us free. For if you refuse to act kindly, you can hardly expect to be treated kindly. Kind mercy wins over harsh judgment every time (James 2:8,12-13 The Message).

In other words, mercy trumps judgment every time. It's amazing how quickly we can judge another's sin because it's different from ours. So, be kind. Be merciful. Love abundantly. Leave the judging to the One who sits on the throne.

Who are you to pass judgment on the servant of another?
It is before his own master that he stands or falls. And he
will be upheld, for the Lord is able to make him stand"(Romans 14:4 ESV).

I encourage you to read the whole 14th chapter of Romans
in the Amplified Bible. I got under conviction, again, reading
this while working on this subject of judging. It's a powerful, straight-to-the-point teaching from the apostle Paul. He
reminds us that it's before God we will give an account, not
other people.

A TONGUE THAT ARGUES

A Negative Tongue

As for the one who is weak in faith, welcome him, but not
to quarrel over opinions (Romans 14:1 ESV).

But avoid foolish and ignorant disputes, knowing that
they generate strife. And a servant of the Lord must
not quarrel but be gentle to all, able to teach, patient
(2 Timothy 2:23-24).

A continual dripping on a very rainy day and a conten-
tious woman are alike (Proverbs 27:15).

Some definitions for "arguing" are quarrelsome, dispute,
combative, antagonistic. My mom used to use the word "cantankerous" when she would talk about a certain person's
personality. In other words, this person liked to argue about
everything. You name it! She would argue about it.

When Paul and I were young in the Lord, there were two
couples who would come to our home almost every night. We
would send our children to one of the bedrooms to play, and
we would get out the Bible and start reading and discussing.

We were all young believers, so we were ignorant of God's Word, yet we argued over Scripture. There were many nights one of the men would leave angry and upset, but the next night we would all be back reading and discussing and hungry to know God's Word. We were like iron sharpening iron. We grew in the Lord, even though we disagreed on some things. What's amazing is that these two couples are still our friends today. We talk about those times of discussion with great fondness. Praise God we grew to where we didn't argue but discussed and exhorted each other in the Lord.

It's amazing how quickly a quarrel can end between two people when one chooses to be quiet! When there's a quarrel, very little is accomplished. Everyone wants their own way. Everyone feels they are right. Let's face it, we all want our own way, but is this pleasing to our Lord? We can agree to disagree and still be friends. We don't have to be right about everything, and actually, we aren't always right about everything.

A Positive Tongue

The opposite meaning of quarrelsome or argumentative is peaceable.

> *If it is possible, as far as it depends on you, live at peace with everyone* (Romans 12:18 NIV).

> *Peace I leave with you, My peace I give to you; not as the world gives do I give to you. Let not your heart be troubled, neither let it be afraid* (John 14:27).

When we have peace in our hearts, the peace that passes all understanding, the peace that our Lord gives, we shouldn't want to use our tongues as instruments of destruction or anger.

A TONGUE THAT WHINES

A Negative Tongue

> *And it came to pass after these things that Naboth the Jezreelite had a vineyard which was in Jezreel, next to the palace of Ahab king of Samaria. So Ahab spoke to Naboth, saying, "Give me your vineyard that I may have it for a vegetable garden, because it is near, next to my house; and for it I will give you a vineyard better than it. Or, if it seems good to you, I will give you its worth in money." But Naboth said to Ahab, "The Lord forbid that I should give the inheritance of my fathers to you!"*
>
> *So Ahab went into his house sullen and displeased because of the word which Naboth the Jezreelite had spoken to him; for he had said, "I will not give you the inheritance of my fathers." And he lay down on his bed, and turned away his face, and would eat no food. But Jezebel his wife came to him, and said to him, "Why is your spirit so sullen that you eat no food?"*
>
> *He said to her, "Because I spoke to Naboth the Jezreelite, and said to him, 'Give me your vineyard for money; or else, if it pleases you, I will give you another vineyard for it.' And he answered, 'I will not give you my vineyard'"*
> (1 Kings 21:1-6).

When I read these verses, I almost laughed. I could just see this man with his thumb in his mouth, his lips in a pout, or a pacifier in his mouth whining about not getting his way. Here's a king, a grown man, lying on his bed, his face toward the wall, refusing to eat...pouting! I can see this picture in my mind's eye. Ahab didn't get his way. He wanted another man's property.

When Naboth said he would never part with what God had given him, Ahab went home and started pouting and whining to his wife. Do you know anyone like this? I sure do! Actually, I've acted like this before; I'm sad to say. I believe we have all acted this way at times when we didn't get our way. Let's act like a spoiled child and see if we can get our way, or whine long enough until someone takes care of the situation for us!

If you read on in the chapter, Ahab's wife told him to get up, cheer up, stop pouting, eat something, and she would take care of the situation. I'm sure Ahab had planned for his wife to see him and do something to help his situation. We want our spouse to take notice of our unhappiness, pouting, and or sulking in order to get our way. Oh, she took care of it all right. She had Naboth murdered so Ahab could have his vineyard. This resulted in God's judgment.

So, how should we respond when we don't get our way?

A Positive Tongue

The opposite of "whine" is defined as: praise, delight, rejoice. The following verses are from The Message Bible because I think we understand this truth best in today's language:

> *And if someone takes unfair advantage of you, use the occasion to practice the servant life. No more tit-for-tat stuff. Live generously. You're familiar with the old written law, "Love your friend," and its unwritten companion, "Hate your enemy." I'm challenging that. I'm telling you to love your enemies. Let them bring out the best in you, not the worst. When someone gives you a hard time, respond with the energies of prayer, for then you are working out of your true selves, your God-created selves.*
>
> *This is what God does. He gives his best—the sun to warm and the rain to nourish—to everyone, regardless:*

the good and bad, the nice and nasty. If all you do is love the lovable, do you expect a bonus? Anybody can do that. If you simply say hello to those who greet you, do you expect a medal? Any run-of-the-mill sinner does that.

In a word, what I'm saying is, Grow up. You're kingdom subjects. Now live like it. Live out your God-created identity. Live generously and graciously toward others, the way God lives toward you (Matthew 5:42-48 The Message).

These are just a few of the ways we use our tongue to either encourage or discourage someone.

Recently I placed an order for some goodies to be delivered to friends who were remembering a loved one who had gone to Heaven. The person who took my order said it would be delivered the day I wanted it delivered. However, I received a shipping notice that day after it was supposed to be delivered saying, "Your package is on its way!" On its way? I called the company to ask about my order. They weren't sure what happened. I couldn't get the man I was talking with to give me the right information. I was really getting frustrated! I wanted to lash out at him. I wanted to give him a piece of my mind over the phone.

But as I was talking to him, the Scriptures I've used about controlling our tongues came to mind. I said to myself, *Practice what you preach!* A pastor friend used to say, "Walk your talk or zip your lip!" I zipped my lip! *"People may be pure in **their own eyes,** but the Lord examines their motives"* (Proverbs 16:2 New Living Translation).

Words are not simply sounds caused by air passing through our larynx. Words have real power. God spoke the world into being by the power of His words (Hebrews 11:3), and we are in His image in part because of the power we have with words. Words do more than convey information. The power of our words can actually destroy someone's spirit, even stir up hatred and violence. They not only exacerbate wounds but inflict them directly. Of all the creatures on this planet, only man has the ability to communicate through the spoken word. The power to use words is a unique and powerful gift from God.

Our words have the power to destroy and the power to build up (Proverbs 12:6). The writer of Proverb tells us, "The tongue has the power of life and death, and those who love it will eat its fruit" (Proverbs 18:21). Are we using words to build up people or destroy them? Are they filled with hate or love, bitterness or blessing, complaining or compliments, lust or love, victory or defeat? Like tools they can be used to help us reach our goals or to send us spiraling into a deep depression.

Furthermore, our words not only have the power to bring us death or life in this world, but in the next as well. Jesus said, "But I tell you that men will have to give account on the day of judgment for every careless word they have spoken. For by your words you will be acquitted, and by your words you will be condemned" (Matthew 12:36-37). Words are so important, that we are going to give an account of what we say when we stand before the Lord Jesus Christ.[3]

In his "10 Disciplines of a Godly Man, R. Kent Hughes writes,

The true test of a man's spirituality is not his ability to speak, as we are apt to think, but rather his ability to bridle his tongue.[4]

Words are powerful; however, there are silent languages called nonverbal communication: body language and tone. Research has found that we assign 55 percent of the weight to body language, 38 percent to tone, and 7 percent to actual words. In other words, our facial expressions speak volumes about our attitude. For example, we can express ourselves by rolling our eyes, folding our arms across our chest, turning our bodies when we don't want to hear what's being said, and on and on.

I was astounded when I read this, as I have always thought that verbal language carried the most weight. However, when I think about some of the times I have used nonverbal language in my communication with people, especially my family, I truly believe nonverbal is powerful. I would guide my children when they were younger by just looking at them in a certain way. I would nod my head and lift my eyebrows, which meant, you better obey or else! I would disagree with Paul by giving him a certain look…no words, just a look! He can read my face. You know what I'm talking about because we all speak in this nonverbal language.

You can discern if a person is not interested in your conversation by their body language. A person doesn't have to be smart to have discernment. I can look in a person's eyes (Matthew 6:22) when I'm speaking to them and know if they are listening to me. It's not rocket science! The eyes speak volumes, as does body language.

I read that, "Ninety percent of the friction of everyday life is caused by the wrong tone of voice." I definitely agree. We can say, "I didn't mean it that way," but our tone gives us away. A person can say, "I'm sorry" and then say, "I said I was sorry" in a tone that can't be mistaken! As husband and wife, we know each other. Paul can ask me, "What's wrong, Hon?" I can say, "Nothing." Let me tell you, he knows I don't mean that. He knows there's something wrong by watching my mannerisms, hearing my tone of voice, and by my look.

But this doesn't mean we don't have to think about what we say.

Words are powerful. They can't be taken back once they are out of our mouths. You've heard the saying, "Sticks and stones may break my bones, but words can never hurt me." Such a lie! Words do so much damage, and some people never get over harsh and cutting words that have been spoken to them.

Use your words wisely and kindly. You don't want to be like the woman who is talked about in Proverbs 11:22: *"As a ring of gold in a swine's snout, so is a lovely woman who lacks discretion."* No matter how beautiful a woman is, if her speech and actions lack discretion—behavior, judgment, taste, understanding— the Scripture says it's like putting a gold ring in a pig's nose. It just doesn't look good, and it doesn't fit!

As women of God, we want this to be our speech; *"She opens her mouth with wisdom, and on her tongue is the law of kindness"* (Proverbs 31:26).

> *We flatter those we scarcely know*
> *We please the fleeting guest*
> *And deal full many a thoughtless blow*
> *To those who love us best.*
> —Ella Wheeler Wilcox

Bob Newhart, the actor, has a hilarious skit on YouTube where he plays a psychiatrist. A woman comes in with a fear of being buried in a box, plus other fears and situations. When Bob hears her out, he simply shouts out, "STOP IT!" Everything she brings up he says the same thing, "STOP IT!" Now, it's a very funny skit, but I say the same thing Bob Newhart says when women say they can't stop talking negatively to their husbands, "STOP IT!" It's a bad habit that can be broken, and it grieves the heart of God. It's not "I can't" but "I won't."

I can do all things through Christ who strengthens me (Philippians 4:13).

ENDNOTES

1. Lehman Strauss, *James Your Brother* (Neptune, NJ: Loizeaux Brothers, 1970), 133.
2. "What is the difference between discernment and being judgmental?" https://bible.org/question/what-difference-between-discernment-and-being-judgmental; accessed August 19, 2018.
3. "What does the Bible say about the power of words?"; https://www.gotquestions.org/power-of-words.html; accessed August 20, 2018.
4. R. Kent Hughes, "10 Disciplines of a Godly Man"; https://www.crossway.org/articles/10-disciplines-of-a-godly-man/; accessed August 29, 2018.

Part IV

Submission

*A*SUBMISSIVE PERSON IS NOT CANTANKEROUS, ASSERTIVE, pushy, self-willed, and difficult to get along with. Believers are to be growing in humility, gentleness, patience, forbearance, and love (Eph. 4:2). Our lives are to be under the control of the Holy Spirit, who produces joy and thankfulness (Eph. 5:18-20). Both those in positions of authority (in the church and home) and those under authority are to be marked by the fruit of the Spirit (Gal. 5:22-23). This puts a check on authoritarian, self-serving, insensitive leadership.[1]

> *Submission to your husband*
> *Can be a funny thing*
> *But it's not a joking matter*
> *For the blessings it can bring*
>
> *That word has often suffered*
> *From the way it's been misused*
> *It's a tragedy for the women*
> *Who have often been abused*
>
> *Abused by words that hurt them*
> *With acts and unkind deeds*
> *And things that scar so deeply*

Only grace can meet their needs

But I know the ones who trust The Lord
Will always stand the test
They'll be protected by God's grace
As they strive to give their best

She has godly worth and beauty
And a heart to do what's right
Her value brings her endless praise
She's PRICELESS in God's sight

—Paul E. Tsika 1/8/2019

Chapter 11

I'm Not Your Concubine

The definition of a concubine is a woman who cohabits with a man to whom she is not legally married, especially one regarded as socially or sexually subservient; mistress; (among polygamous peoples) a secondary wife, usually of inferior rank.[2]

So, what is a concubine? In the Old Testament, it was common for a man to have many concubines. Yes, God allowed this but it doesn't mean He condoned or approved it. A concubine could be taken without any of the ceremonies or benefits of a marriage relationship. All a man needed were the resources and desire to own one. The position was that of a slave or servant and she was always considered inferior to a wife.

The law required a concubine to provide sex for her master and to have and raise the children. She was also expected to wash his clothes, wash the dishes, clean the house, cook his meals, plus any other duties he wished her to fulfill. She had none of the privileges or inheritance that a wife had. There was no obligation on the part of the man to provide emotional or relational support—no genuine love.

Do you sometimes feel like a concubine? Do you sometimes feel like you provide all of these services but without love, honor, or respect from your husband? Do you feel like you are doing all the giving and he's doing all the taking?

You may have felt, or still feel, like a concubine. I've heard women say, "I am so lonely. I feel like my husband doesn't even know I exist. He comes home late from work, eats dinner, falls asleep on the couch, then gets up and goes to bed. He doesn't meet my needs emotionally, spiritually, or physically." These women are ready to scream or just leave because the void in their hearts grow every day. The husbands say, "We're doing great. I don't know why she's feeling this way. I'm working hard to provide for our family. I tell her I'm doing this for her. What more can I do?" What's the problem here?

Many marriages start off on the wrong foot. It's broken from the beginning because the man and woman were selfishly using each other to fulfill their own needs and desires. So as the years go on, the problem escalates. The husband feels like his wife is a nag if she asks him to change. The wife feels like her husband is too domineering if he asks her to change. Is this too much to ask? No! We should all be changing as we grow older together. Can we change each other? No, but we can pray for each other, love each other, and encourage each other in the right way. When we do, God will change us and show us how to be better spouses to each other.

Paul and I have changed dramatically through the years. Thank God, we didn't stay the same. Did we want to change? Not so much in the early years. In the beginning, I'm sure Paul thought I should do all the changing, and I felt he needed to do all the changing. And of course, I was right. Just kidding!

However, as we grew older, and God "intruded" into our lives, we both knew we had lots of changing to do.

WORTH IT? ABSOLUTELY!

We were at our granddaughter's wedding, and the question was asked, "How did you two make your marriage last for fifty-two years?" My answer—there was a lot of forgiveness, love, and commitment. Paul agreed, but he said he should have added, "and a good woman who will be patient enough for her husband to grow up." Easy? Absolutely not! Worth it? Absolutely!

I've always said that *submission is an attitude of the heart.* There's an old saying, "I may be standing on the outside, but I'm sitting on the inside." This isn't submission. I believe women are seeking answers to life. Women are shouting, "I want my rights." We want equality and liberation, and many believe this is the avenue of fulfillment. However, there are those who have discovered that Christ, and Christ alone, is the only One who can fill that void in their heart.

There are those who say it's all about a man's macho ego, so we have to give in and let him have his way to pacify him. No, it's about our place, or duty, according to God's Word. We have an authority over us that God placed in our lives to protect and lead us. This is a good thing. This doesn't mean we are not equal or that we are of less value; God's Word says that we are the weaker vessel. Read First Peter chapter 3 in the Amplified Bible to get the whole picture. You may argue with me, but you can't argue with God. His Word is truth!

Now, please don't shut me out because of this word "submission." So many of us thought of this word or still think of this word as a negative. However, it seems we balk at this word only when it's talking about submission to our husbands. We bow up! We are determined never to let a man tell us what to do, how to live, how to dress, or where to go. We are not going to be bossed by our husbands. We are not going to be controlled by them. Listen, I understand. *I am a woman!* I am Eve's daughter, as is every woman on the face of this earth.

For many years, I had the wrong concept of submission. I didn't feel like I had the right to speak up or share my opinions with Paul; and yes, he felt the same way. He was the boss and couldn't be questioned. I let Paul rule over me as though I was his child rather than his wife and equal to him. He felt like he could talk to me and treat me any way he wanted, and I didn't have the right to disagree with him. So, we were both wrong on this issue of submission. We both interpreted the word "helpmeet" wrong. It took devastation in our marriage to awaken both of us to the true meaning of submission and understand the powerful position of a helpmeet.

I remember telling Paul, after our position on submission changed, that I submit to him because I choose to, not because he forces me to. I submit because I know this is right in God's sight and His Word makes it plain that I should. A man can't make a woman submit. It's a choice she makes to be obedient to God's Word and honor her husband. It's a matter of the heart. Does this make her inferior to her husband? Absolutely not! This is her place of protection.

I asked a lot of women to give me their thoughts on submission. My daughter, Gretchen, sent the following to me:

> Submission: I really didn't like it, for several reasons. First, I wanted to do my own thing, my own way, and in my own time. Why should anyone, least of all my husband, tell me what to do, when to do it, and how to do it? Second, when I was growing up, I felt that maybe I had a skewed view of this. My mama was and still is an amazing wife and mama, but I saw her do

everything my dad said without question, and I feel like she just did it because she was supposed to submit to him because the Bible said to. I didn't see her ever question my dad or try to get her own way. She just did what he said.

Now, I'm not saying that is entirely wrong, but I do feel like even she had a skewed view of submission. After twenty-plus years together, I did see this change. I think she realized that submission isn't a man dominating his authority over his wife and she just saying yes dear to everything. Submission is a wife coming under the submission and authority of her husband *as the husband* comes under the submission and authority of the Lord *first!*

As I saw this change in my mama and I was trying to navigate the waters of my own marriage, I realized that submission can be and is an amazing thing. It certainly lets me have the freedom to be who I am and have my say in our marriage. I feel like the husband actually has the harder role in this. He has to submit to the Lord and really doesn't get to question but has to fully trust and believe in the sovereignty of the Lord.

This gives me great peace knowing that my husband is in submission to the Lord and will do the best for our marriage. As he is in submission and truly following the Lord, I have no problem submitting to him. Does he ask and value my opinion? Absolutely! Does he sometimes realize that I may have a better idea when we are trying to solve an issue? Yes, he does. That doesn't mean that I don't question, because I do, or get a bad attitude at times, because I do, or not always agree, because I don't. But ultimately, if he feels like what he is doing and saying is in direct submission to the Lord, I faithfully and gladly submit to him.

—Gretchen Ann Rush, age 51, married 30 years

Gretchen has it right, as I shared earlier in my confession about my skewed view of submission. I believe most women would agree with us when it comes to having a bad attitude at times when we don't get our way in a situation. I still battle this from time to time, and I've been married more than fifty years.

Genesis 2:18 says, *"And the Lord God said, "It is not good that man should be alone; I will make him a helper* [ay'zer] *comparable to him."*

This word "helper" or "helpmeet," is a powerful word that is used in other verses of the Bible speaking about God being our help: *"O Israel, trust in the Lord; He is their help* [ay'zer] *and their shield"* (Psalm 115:9); *"Our soul waits for the Lord; He is our help* [ay'zer] *and our shield"* (Psalm 33:20); *"Happy is he who has the God of Jacob for his help* [ay'zer], *whose hope is in the Lord his God"* (Psalm 146:5).

The word "help" in these verses is talking about our Lord being our help in time of need. The very same meaning as *help-meet* when it speaks of our position as a wife. How amazing is that! How desperately we need the Lord in every area of our lives! We need Him to encourage us. We need Him to be our strength and refuge. We need Him in times of trouble. We need Him to protect us. We need Him at all times—the same way a husband needs his wife to be his "help" at all times. Our role, as a wife, is vital.

I use the Amplified Bible to cite the next few verses because I like the way it states the truth about our role as wives. These are not suggestions from God but commands. It's our duty as godly Christian women to submit to those God has put in authority over us. Let me reiterate, they are *not* suggestions! They are commands! God didn't say love Him with all your heart, mind, and soul if you feel like it. He didn't say submit to your husbands as you do toward Me if you feel like it. This is the world's view, not God's!

> *Wives, be subject to your husbands [out of respect for their position as protector, and their accountability to God], as is proper and fitting in the Lord* (Colossians 3:18 AMP).

> *Wives, be subject to your own husbands, as [a service] to the Lord. For the husband is head of the wife, as Christ is head of the church, Himself being the Savior of the body. But as the church is subject to Christ, so also wives should be subject to their husbands in everything [respecting both their position as protector and their responsibility to God as head of the house]* (Ephesians 5:22-24 AMP).

> *In the same way, you wives, be submissive to your own husbands [subordinate, not as inferior, but out of respect for the responsibilities entrusted to husbands and their accountability to God, and so partnering with them] so that even if some do not obey the word [of God], they may be won over [to Christ] without discussion by the godly lives of their wives, when they see your modest and respectful behavior [together with your devotion and appreciation—love your husband, encourage him, and enjoy him as a blessing from God]* (1 Peter 3:1-2 AMP).

The admonition Peter gives us in this Scripture passage begins with, *"In the same way."* So, this means there were instructions that Peter gave before he begins with our role as wives. His admonition is to all Christians. He starts by saying,

"Because of God's abundant and boundless mercy we are born again." We are spiritually transformed, renewed, and set apart for His purpose. We have an ever-living hope, and we can be assured, because of the resurrection of Jesus Christ, we have an inheritance that is imperishable and undefiled and unfading and reserved in Heaven for us. "Born again" means we are new babies in Christ. We need to be cared for and taught how to act and live.

Peter says to put aside our old life and be holy—pure, morally blameless, sacred. We are a chosen generation, a royal priesthood, a holy nation, a peculiar people, so we should show this in our manner of life. We were not like this in our past life, but we have obtained mercy from our Father, so let's live a godly life. He goes on to tell us to submit to every ordinance of man for the Lord's sake—kings, presidents, governors—in other words, those who have authority over us. He says that servants should be submissive to their masters; we can relate this to our day as employees should be submissive to their employers.

I have a very dear friend, Rosie Brieden, who is ninety-two years of age. She is in a home where I can visit her often. She and her husband, Elmer, who is in Heaven, lived on a dairy farm and raised six children. My brother and I spent many days at the farm, so we were like her children. I call her my second mom.

I visited Rosie while writing this chapter on submission, so I asked her point of view on this subject. She is from another generation, so I thought maybe her views would be a little bit different from today's generation. Rosie said, "I just did what Elmer told me to do." Now, Elmer was an easy guy to get along with, which makes it a lot easier to submit. However, he could be stubborn! His refusal to travel away from the farm would frustrate Rosie, as she wanted to go visit people or travel a little. She said she would get so mad at him, but then she would get over it because she knew she couldn't change his mind by being angry.

Should Elmer have considered her desires? Yes, but he didn't. So, for her to stay angry about his refusal to travel would have been futile. She adapted her life to his, which is biblical (see 1 Peter 3:5 Amplified Bible). I know today's generation has been indoctrinated by the world's point of view or Hollywood's stand, portrayed in the movies, on submission when it comes to a wife being in submission. However, the truth hasn't changed.

The Bible isn't some old book that's out of date. The following are just as true today as they were in biblical times.

What do husbands want from their wives?

- Respect!
- Not speaking to them like they're children.
- Not treating them like children; he didn't marry his mother.
- Not questioning their authority.
- Never saying, "You need to be like so and so, then I will respect you."
- Never belittling what he has provided.
- Never correcting him in public. ("No, honey, it was Monday, not Tuesday. It was 1:15 not 2 o'clock. May I tell you something? No one cares what day or what time things happened. It's the meaning behind what's being told.")
- Keeping a clean house.
- Respecting him above other men.
- Appreciating his hard work.

- Never interfering when he disciplines the children.

VIEWS ON THE WORD "SUBMISSION"

God called Paul and me into a marketplace ministry in 2001. Paul is the pastor to approximately 130,000 people. This organization calls us their spiritual advisors, even though most of the business owners have their own church and pastor. Many in this organization are Christians. So, I asked some of the women in this organization to share with me their views on this topic of submission. I also asked my daughter, daughters-in-law, and granddaughters to provide me their views.

I am so proud of all of these women who have come to a biblical understanding of submission. I had to laugh at some of them because I remember my younger days of wrong thinking and my struggle to be the kind of wife who wanted to please the Lord. However, we never get too old to learn. I believe I'm learning more in my older years than I did when I was young. The following are their views.

When I first heard "wives submit to your husbands," I actually got angry. I am a young woman in business and I fully believe that women can do big, amazing, earthshaking things without "submitting" to a man. But what I have learned is that the world's definition of the word "submit" is really, really different from what God's definition is. I used to think that submitting to your husband meant forfeiting your rights, opinions, feelings, and ideas to go along with whatever your husband said and did. You would have no control and basically be ruled over. Women were number two and really just of no value—once you married a man you had to submit to him! Yep. *Not cool!* Good thing this isn't actually the case, but the world's view of submission definitely made it seem that way to me!

Now I know what God was really saying with that Scripture passage. Marriage is a covenant with the man as the leader, yes, *but*...it definitely does not mean you can't have an opinion and have to be under the power of a man forever and ever! God also says, *"Husbands love your wives as Christ loves the church."* That statement sounds really simple until you think about it. God wants your husband, or future husband, to love you just like Christ loves the Church. Do you know how stinkin' much that is?!?!

—Shelby Tsika, granddaughter, age 22, engaged

I had never heard the word "submission" until I got in the business. I was single when I started building, so most of the time it went over my head when I heard audios and speakers mention the "s" word. I got saved, then married within eight months of that, which to me meant that I would have to be a submissive wife. Logically, I knew it was the right thing to do, to let my husband lead, to go under his mission, but it was extremely difficult, even after all the Christian books I read on marriage. It wasn't until my *heart* changed through much prayer, that it became easy.

Submission, to me, means humility, trust, respect and strength, both in marriage and outside of marriage—child to parent, student to teacher, etc.

—Sandee Tsuruda, married 26 years

When I first heard the word "submission," I thought of a doormat, someone who others walk all over, someone who is weak and can't stand up for themselves. Now I know this is not true. When I think of submission in marriage, I think of conforming or yielding to my husband's will or desire. In a good marriage, I believe there is submission both ways.

However, the husband is the God-given leader and head in the marriage, which means he gets the final say. For me this means practicing selflessness; not having to have it my way. This is not always easy to do, especially with a choleric personality. So, when I am successful at being submissive, it is usually because I have applied the following:

1. Prayer—giving all things over to God; I pray especially for my husband that God will give him wisdom in his burden of being accountable to make the right choices.

Also, I pray for myself. Repent when necessary and pray for the right heart and attitude when I am not getting my way.

2. Be quiet, hold my tongue. This has helped me a lot. Taking my thoughts captive to God is so necessary because I am also a sanguine personality and tend to speak my mind.

I love that submission is such a powerful action that can win others to Christ, even husbands, and that submission in marriage shows reverence for Christ.

These to me are the main reasons to be submissive.

—Sandy Sears, age 58, married 36 years

I gave my life to Christ at twenty-seven years of age. When I then studied marriage, I realized how important it would be to find a man who truly fears the Lord and was submitted to him. I learned that God made both men and women in His image—equal. Yet in marriage, He wanted the wife to be submitted to her husband in everything and the husband submitted to the Lord. Husbands are to love their wives as Jesus loves the church and gave Himself up for the church. Husbands are also responsible to present their wives as holy, covering her with the washing with water through the Word and must love their wife as he loves his own body. (No pressure for the husbands…lol.)

With this illustration, it is a totally secure and peaceful place for wives to be in submission to their husbands. Knowing this, I wanted it and waited on the Lord to bring me my husband. I did not date and waited for six years. I wanted God to bring me a husband who knew Him, loved Him, and was grounded in the Word. (Crazy faith…lol.) And He did. Howie and I accepted Christ on the same day.

Howie and I have now been married twenty-one years. Have we always agreed? No. Have we had our shares of disagreements and arguments? Yes. Yet through it all, I trust Howie's heart. He is a man of integrity and loves me and fears the Lord. I am truly blessed and am honored to be in submission to Howie's mission: To honor God, serve people, and love people and our family.

Submission: To be submitted to one's calling and mission. I am blessed and honored to be in submission to Howie Danzik.

—Theresa Danzik

⸎

When I think of submission, the words "honor" and "respect" come to the forefront of my mind. Under one's mission, respectfully and honorably demonstrating in all ways my value and position toward whomever I am blessed to be in submission to.

—Leslie Wolgamott Rice, age 54, married 2 years

⸎

God put another strong-willed woman on this earth the day I was born. My particular personality has provided me with the immediate and continuous opportunity to experience the challenge and beauty of submission over and over again. My understanding of the idea of submission begins and ends in my relationship with a loving God.

I remember as a little girl having a sense of profound frustration when things weren't going the way I wanted them to. Even as a small, strong-willed lady, I believed that I knew best; that my plans were in everyone's best interest—that had to be the case because I could hold on really hard to a good plan. The results of living according to my plans have been very clear looking back. I've left a trail of hurtful conversations, broken friendships, mistrust, and the consequences of sinful choices in my wake.

The first Bible study I did on the topic of submission in marriage was tough. I was in my mid-twenties and didn't think that I should submit to my husband unless he deserved it. He hadn't particularly shown himself worthy, so I packed that topic away. What I have learned is that biblical submission doesn't stay packed away. It screams at the top of its lungs to be heard and understood and practiced.

As a woman at the age of fifty-three,, I continue to discover the challenge and beauty of the kind of submission that God has ordained. He has loved me so much that He continues to give me opportunities to live out biblical submission to Him and to other people. Here's what He has taught me so far.

If I hold my plans in abeyance—suspension, remission, or dormancy—to God's perfect agenda, that act of submission allows me to remember that I have asked God to be completely in charge of my life and I am serious about that. Isaiah 55:8-9 explains that God's thoughts and ways are absolutely higher than mine that there is no way my plans could ever trump His. His plans are good, perfect, trustworthy, and dependable. I can and should wake up each day watching as His plan is revealed in my life.

Because I have chosen to submit myself to God, I get to practice being in submission to others in authority in my life, including my husband. This type of submission is a position of such strength. I get to go beyond my emotions in the moment and believe God has a higher and better way, and then act in faith. As I write these words, I am thinking how easy it sounds and how very hard it can be at times; and that is why biblical submission requires me to be on my knees asking God for the strength to bow.

—Bobbi Puryear, age 53

I have struggled with submission, definitely. It's easy to tell yourself that you are in submission when things are going your way and you can agree on things. However, that doesn't reveal the heart. When you don't see eye to eye on things, when circumstances of life are hard and challenging—that's when self-ishness surfaces. My faith and numerous humbling moments have set me back on the path. Most of the humbling moments are when I see later on that I was just flat-out wrong. Or worse yet, when I hurt my husband, when he sees me acting out "this is just how I am, there's no room for change so just accept me as I am." Ouch.

—Noella Olynyk, age 33, married 11 years

Because there was not only love but also respect in our marriage, it was easy for me to be in submission to my husband. I not only wanted him to be but also needed him to be the leader of our family and our home.

—Georgia Lee Puryear

Submission is a woman's strength, when to say something or when to just pray…. And to understand God has it all figured out already.

—Sandy Yuen, age 55, married 27 years

For the heck of it, I looked up the definition of "submission" on Google to see what the world thinks submission means before I put in my two cents: "The action or act of accepting or yielding to a superior force or to the will or authority of another person."

I think the line "yielding to a superior force" is what throws women off these days, just like it did me for so many years. I grew up telling myself that I would be a strong, independent woman who didn't need someone else to basically control my life to survive. For so many years when I heard these words at weddings, "submit to your husband," I immediately pictured a weak woman kneeling in front of her husband like a servant who would do anything to be loved because that is what was "expected" of her by the husband. Up until Demetri and I met up with you and Pawpaw at the bay house for one of our first counseling sessions, I knew the word "submission" to be a negative word.

After you and Pawpaw explained more clearly what submission meant in the Bible, my opinion quickly changed. Now when I hear the words, "submit to your husband," I picture a strong, selfless woman who would do anything for her husband, for the better of course, because of her desire to love him and care for him. It wasn't until we got married and were living together that I realized the pure joy that it gives me to do things for Demetri that he doesn't necessarily ask for or expect me to do because I'm his wife, but because I want to show him that I'm always looking out for him no matter what time of day it is.

One interesting thing that I'm starting to see going into our seventh month of marriage is that the more I submit to Demetri, he also submits to me and wants to serve me because of the way I treat him in the first place. It's basically this amazing circle that we're running in that I know will only get stronger because of our desire to serve one another by submitting ourselves to the other. It's amazing how relationships can change when you ignore the "definition" and open yourself up to understanding what God intended submission to be in a marriage.

—Kaleigh Tsika, age 25, married
1 year to our grandson

I can honestly say, that until about twenty years ago, I never heard of the word "submission." I was a new business builder at a conference, and a new business partner of mine came up to me with distain on her face asking me about the word "submission." Apparently, a speaker talked about the word and this gal was not happy. I could not answer her. I didn't even look the word up. However, I did hear the word a few more times at the business event, and I remember hearing someone saying it meant "subject to the mission." I could swallow that, however, it seemed to bother some of my stronger women teammates.

As I asked a few people why that word was so upsetting to them, I heard a common theme—that my husband rules me; he makes all the decisions without me; I am "under him." Again, I had trouble answering their grievances, but clearly it was a real thing and I couldn't discount it. All I could share was how Tracey and I chose to operate concerning our marriage, business, and submission.

I must admit, when we were first married, I was the one who made all the major decisions. My mom was quite strong and that was the best example I had And honestly, it worked in our marriage for a little while and Tracey was ok with that. After a few years, Tracey wanted to become the leader of our home and we had to make adjustments. I wasn't really liking that. It wasn't a major struggle, but certainly I thought we could lead equally. That caused quite a few arguments. I guess I wasn't ready to give up that power, so to speak; and honestly, I thought I could make better decisions due to my insight, etc. So clearly, I didn't trust him and that was unfortunate. It wasn't his fault. I just wasn't ready for the change.

So, I basically handed over the reins. But of course I wanted to be intrinsically part of all the decision making, and I could tell it was really bothering him, which caused many drag-down arguments. I heard someone talk about the book *Wild at Heart* by John Eldredge and the book *Finding the Hero in Your Husband* by Julianna Slattery. In fact, I had *Finding the*

Hero in Your Husband on my nightstand and Tracey asked, "Why are you reading that? Am I not your hero?" It was at that moment everything clicked for me. He looked like such a little boy and all he wanted to do is lead our family, rescue the maiden (me) and be the hero. My heart melted and I began to change. It wasn't important for me to make all the decisions anymore. In fact, I asked him not to ask my input unless he really, really wanted it. Trust me, I had to bite my lip so many times, and it was so hard not to keep a scorecard when I felt it was the wrong direction for our family.

Here's what I found, though, since I trusted him. Even when things didn't go well, he began to ask for my input. He felt like the leader. He felt encouraged and respected…and he trusted me.

So, submission to me is allowing my husband to lead so we can today have a really cool, trusting dynamic in our family. He now asks me constantly for my input, but even if he doesn't implement it, I'm so happy he asked.

And finally, now that I've been watching him lead our family for many years now, I am so grateful it is not me. He has had to make so many difficult decisions, that honestly, I'm sure I couldn't emotionally handle. And, I think the pressure over time would have been way too much. I see so many stressed out women trying to do it all and make all the major decisions, and I see them slowly, over time, lose respect for their husband and they look exhausted. I heard once, "You can have it all, just not at the same time." I believe God designed me for a very special assignment and that assignment has been to help and support my man, and it's been such a pleasure watching him mature and grow into the man he is today. He is definitely the hero to our children. What more could you want? We are equal, but not the same. That is for sure.

—Kimberly Eaton, age 50, married 26 years

One of the best definitions of submission I've ever heard is "submitted to his vision" or submitted to your vision as a couple. I've come to understand that is when you channel your strength and power as a woman and as a total team player in pursuing your dreams together. I've learned that a woman of strength remembers that larger vision in her marriage on a daily basis. That it's not just about our personal happiness, but what if ultimately marriage was more about making us holy than happy? I've also learned that submission means that my husband carries 51 percent of the voting stock on our team, and as a leader he deserves my respect in that role. The fruit of this is that as I've submitted over the years, I've noted my husband has learned he can truly trust me to respect that leadership. And now he has, in turn, asked for more and more of my opinions and insights and has implemented many of them with our business partners and family.

—Ann Golden, age 63, married 34 years

I believe this is where a lot of women are today in their views about submission. I love Karla's truthfulness about wanting her hubby to submit to her because of all she had accomplished on her own. She now realizes that it takes a woman of strength to give over the reins to her husband. This makes for a happy marriage! Well, my view of submission, and what has resonated with me is "under a mission"—God's mission. So, by submitting to Bob I am summiting to God. Is it hard sometimes? Absolutely! Perfect? No! But as Paul says, "progress." I have absolute faith that in submitting, God will reveal His purpose in the moment and down the road. Billie, I know you have said your trailer is hitched to Paul's. I do believe most women really want that, but so many men are taking their wives on a joy ride, not one that has a destination. Every day I pray and trust God, that in honoring Him, it will fill the desires of my heart.

—Shelly Kummer, age 58, married 30 years

I used to view submission as me placating my husband and that I was obliged to accept his decisions not from a joyful and willing spirit, but from an obliged one because that was what I was "supposed" to do. Now, I view submission as a beautiful act, delighting when my husband takes initiative and responsibility to lead our family. It's not me leaving my brain at the altar or agreeing with everything my husband says, but it *is* me choosing to yield to his leadership—as long as he is not leading me to sin—as I believe God has placed him as the spiritual head of our home.

—Marcie Whalen, age 35, married 10 years

The first thing that comes to mind about submission is, biblically speaking: being my husband's helpmeet, meaning following his vision for our family and being on his team 100 percent; no matter whether I agree on the method, unless of course it was going against God's Word; loving him where he is and trusting his judgment, because I know his intentions; allowing God to use me if and when needed to help Trevor. Submission does not mean telling him I trust him but then questioning every decision that he makes and trying to share with him why what I think is the better way.

—Lexie Baker, age 34, married 13 years

Submission to me simply means accountability. My desire is to be obedient to the calling on my life and to live a life of significance. Part of that calling is to be in partnership with my husband as a godly couple running through the jungle, holding hands, attacking our vision together. When we come across obstacles in our path, I trust my husband to guide me so we can keep going in the right direction. If

I fight him and try to go another way, it slows down the mission God has already laid out for us.

—Jen Brown, age 53, married 25 years

My interpretation of submission is when husband and wife are going the same direction and are together on the same page. Both make selfless choices to reach their goal. It's a give and take relationship in which a couple lives in consideration of each other as they make decisions for their life together.

As a wife, I am called to be his helpmeet. That means I am submitting to the plan. This can otherwise be stated as undergirding the mission, getting under or behind the mission, and making sure it gets accomplished. I will do what needs to be done to accomplish the mission, even if it might not be what another wife would be expected to do in her marriage. Submission does not mean I am a doormat without an opinion; but after I give my input, I follow the lead of my husband and trust God with the results.

—Melanie Tsika, age 48, married
29 years (daughter-in-law)

I feel that submission is really trusting the Lord by trusting my husband to make the best decisions and to guide our family in whatever it may be. It is not a control thing and it's sad that the word gets turned to be that way. It is a special place for a woman to be aligned with her husband and the Lord.

—Emily Tsika Lewis, age 27, married/
divorced/single (granddaughter)

Submission is choosing to ask what the other person's thoughts are because you care more about the other's view and not just your own. However, it looks different for every marriage and for each person. I think the biggest thing for me is listening to the other person not out of fear or obligation but out of respect for my spouse. I think knowing each other's weaknesses and not using them against each other, but knowing them well enough to get each other through low points. I think humbling yourself and realizing you need each other is important and to not let it be a one-sided marriage. There should be no taking advantage of, and I use obedience slightly, but obedience to God not to your spouse. Having a one-sided argument where one person tries to prove themselves right is never okay.

—Marissa Rush, age 23, single (granddaughter)

In my mind, submission is simply "under one mission." When we got married, we joined hands and Glen was going to lead our family. But I was going to run right alongside him on the field, in the game. We didn't have different goals for our family and our future. We had one mission that we were going to run in life toward. Once we really understood this—and kept the drama and emotion out of it—it created an energy and power. "When two become one" has been very strengthening and rooted.

—Joya Baker, married 38 years

When I hear the word "submission" today, it has a totally different meaning from when I first heard it forty years ago. To be honest, when we became involved in our marketing business and I first heard submission when listening to audios, reading books on our booklist, and attending functions, the "s" word caused me great angst! It still is not my favorite word only because I think it is easily misunderstood and people think it means something it does not.

I originally thought to be in submission to Bill meant I needed to act like his slave and agree with him on everything and never think for myself. That absolutely did not sit well with me. Thank goodness I grew spiritually and personally and soon realized being in submission didn't mean that at all. Fortunately, I am blessed to be married to a godly man who is in submission to our Lord, to God's laws, and to man's laws. He submits to those in authority, which in turn makes it possible for me to submit to him in our marriage. He does value my opinion, and we discuss everything before making major decisions.

But ultimately, if we don't agree, he is the decision maker. What gives me great peace is knowing that he is in submission to God. Because of this, it is possible for me to honor and respect his role as the leader of our family and be a submissive wife. Is it always easy? Do I always do this perfectly? No! But, since Bill is in submission to God, and my goal each day is to live a life that is pleasing to Him, I do my very best to be the submissive wife that God, who in His Word, instructed me to be.

—Sandy Hawkins, age 63, married 42 years

Submission isn't just yielding, it is yielding with a grateful heart. It's knowing that God put a man in your life that He deemed to protect you, lead you, and love you. It is not being a zombie or "bowing down" to your husband. Submission is being equal but knowing that God gave you somebody to make the tough decisions, but that the guy He gave you will consider you in all decisions. It is knowing that even if it is hard, submitting to your husband will be rewarded greatly, in your relationship with him, your children, but mostly with God.

We are called to submit just as Jesus submitted to the church. He loved us the most and gave us an earthly person to give us a glimpse of what that love looks like. We submit because God told us to and because our husbands love us enough to deserve that submission.

—Malory Rush Northrup, age 22, married 1 year *(Granddaughter who wrote this before she got married, so I asked her mom if I need to get her views now—ha!)*

Now that I am seventy-one years of age and have been married to Terry for forty-three years, the word "submission" has a different meaning than it did in my youth. On first hearing the word, my thoughts were that I was being asked to "submit" myself to someone else's control. And that was a hard saying to accept. Then, as a Christian, a Christ follower, I again heard that word as I was being asked to "submit" all that I had and all that I was to God.

I started to understand that as I was in submission to people God asked me to be in submission to, whether it was my husband or a boss or a government official, my act was an act of continuing to honor and submit to God. And life became much more joyful and peaceful. It's all about "letting go and letting God"!

—Linda Felber, age 71, married 43 years

My understanding of a wife's choice to submit to the leadership of her husband is based on what I have learned and adopted from the Bible. In Ephesians 5:22 (NIV), Paul writes, *"Wives, submit yourselves to your own husbands as you do to the Lord."* In other words, as a wife God asks me to come under the leadership of my husband, just as he is to submit to the Lord. When I choose to submit to my husband, it is as if I am submitting to God. It does not mean that I follow blindly and do whatever he tells me to do, it means that I allow him to lead me because God has called him to be the leader of our home.

In Proverbs 31, a wife of noble character is described as her husband having full confidence in her because she brings him good and not harm. She works hard by providing for her family, her husband is well respected, and her husband and children praise her. This sounds like a very successful woman and family, not an insecure woman by any means. My husband respects my intuitions and he uses my input to help him make great decisions. If we disagree, he knows that I will give him the freedom to make the best decisions for our family. If he messes up, he knows that I will extend grace, despite my disappointment, and give him the opportunity to change. I once read that submission means being just low enough so that when God zaps my husband I won't get hit!

—Theresa Attalah, age 51, married 24 years

I can submit when I feel secure, protected, and respected. My husband is a master at all three of these, so submission comes easier.

—Laurie Duncan, married 38 years

Submission can look different on different days. It can be as small as buying the coffee he likes over yours or as big as agreeing to move across the country with him. It's putting each other's needs and wants before our own. There are days when this is easy and, of course, there are those challenging days where being "right" can seem more important. These days don't ever end well! For me, part of submitting is trusting your spouse has your best interest at heart as they are trusting God for direction.

—Kelley Tsika, age 47, married
27 years (daughter-in-law)

My definition of submission: the activation and willing heart to allow my husband to lead by embracing his authority in my life. To relinquish the mindset of "I" and all the selfishness that comes along within that and cultivating the mindset of "we" and becoming more selfless toward my husband and marriage.

—Vanessa Crandall, age 30, married 5 years

Submission is an order for a marriage relationship given from above. For me, submission does not make me any less than my husband in our marriage. Submission just means that I trust and love my husband enough to follow his lead—as well as I trust and love God to obey His commands.

—Paxton Tsika, age 21, married
2 years (grandson's wife)

When it comes to submitting to your husband, I believe that you are putting your full trust in him and knowing that his love for you and God drive his decisions. Like when he says we are going to Krispy Kreme, you don't automatically think it's the devil. You know it's God sent!

—Marlee Kaye Tsika, age 23, single
(Granddaughter who is being silly at the end
of her thoughts on submission, but she has
a great example in her mom, Melanie.)

John Piper wrote the following about submission:

If you bring to the Bible your preconceptions, you might just throw the baby out with the bathwater, and say, "If that's what submission means, then I'm out of here." That would be very sad. You may be right, you may be wrong, but it would be sad. I wrote down six things submission to a husband in marriage is *not:*

1. Submission is not agreeing on everything.

2. Submission does not mean leaving your brain at the altar.

3. Submission does not mean you do not try to influence your husband.

4. Submission is not putting the will of the husband before the will of Christ.

5. Submission does not mean getting all of her spiritual strength through her husband.

6. Submission does not mean living or acting in fear.

Submission is the defined calling of a wife to honor and affirm her husband's leadership, and so help to carry it through according to her gifts.[3]

Be subject for the Lord's sake to every human institution, whether it be to the emperor as supreme, or to governors as sent by him to punish those who do evil and to praise those who do good. For this is the will of God, that by doing good you should put to silence the ignorance of foolish people. Live as people who are free, not using your freedom as a cover-up for evil, but living as servants of God. Honor everyone. Love the brotherhood. Fear God. Honor the emperor.

Servants, be subject to your masters [employers] *with all respect, not only to the good and gentle but also to the unjust. For this is a gracious thing, when, mindful of God, one endures sorrows while suffering unjustly. For what credit is it if, when you sin and are beaten* [unjustly treated] *for it, you endure? But if when you do good and suffer for it you endure this is a gracious thing in the sight of God. For to this you have been called, because Christ also suffered for you, leaving you an example, so that you might follow in his steps* (1 Peter 2:13-21 ESV).

We see in these Scripture verses from First Peter that everyone is under an authority. Submission is a vital part of the Christian life. Whether we like it or not, or agree with it or not, we have authorities over us.

SUBMISSION IS THE KEY

So, what is submission?

Submission is the key to unity and harmony in all human relationships.

Therefore, if there is any encouragement in Christ, any comfort provided by love, any fellowship in the Spirit, any affection or mercy, complete my joy and be of the same mind, by having the same love, being united in spirit, and having one purpose. Instead of being motivated by selfish ambition or vanity, each of you should, in humility, be moved to treat one another as more important than yourself. Each of you should be concerned not only about your own interests, but about the interests of others as well (Philippians 2:1-4).

Satan's fall and his on-going rebellion is a manifestation of his refusal to submit to God; he likewise tempts men to follow in his footsteps. Satan abused his power and position, acting independently of God (see Isaiah 14:14; Ezekiel 28:11-15).[4]

In the Garden, the man was to submit to God by trusting Him. However, Adam and Eve decided they would do what they wanted and ate of the tree God had told them not even to touch, much less eat from (see Genesis 3:3). They refused to submit to God's authority. They wanted their own way.

Submission is not man's idea but God's. Submission is an attitude of the heart. A person may obey, but their heart is far from being submissive. I've heard the saying, "I may be standing on the outside, but I'm sitting on the inside." That's called rebellion; an unwillingness to submit!

I don't believe we get married to destroy each other. I believe we all start out wanting to have a great marriage, a great relationship with our hubby, build a great life together, love each other, and have great success in life.

In Paul's book *The Overcomer's Edge,* he writes about relationships. He quotes Jeff Haden who said:

> Professional success is important to everyone, but still, success in business and in life means different things to different people, as well it should. But one fact is universal: Real success, the kind that exists on multiple levels, is impossible without building great relationships. Real success is impossible unless you treat other people with kindness, regard and respect. After all, you can be a rich jerk...but you will also be a lonely jerk.[5]

I agree with Haden, but I will add that it must start in the home. If we don't treat our spouse with kindness and respect and have regard for him, what we do and say outside the home is a "farce." Kindness and respect must start in the home. What good is money, fame, accolades from friends, going to church, reading your Bible, praying, or having popularity if your home is in a mess of constant turmoil and strife?

The greatest relationship outside of Christ should be with our husbands and then our children. Yes, I put your husband in front of your children. He must come first. Remember, your children are going to grow up, find mates, start their own lives without mom and dad, and have their own children. We, as parents, aren't the most important people in their lives, anymore. I know it's hard to swallow, but it's true. Ask any parent whose children have "flown the coop"! This is why our relationship with our spouse is vital.

In Exodus chapter 20, God gave us the Ten Commandments. The first four pertain to our love, respect, honor, and commitment to God and the next six tell us how to treat each other as human beings. However, there were hundreds of laws given for the people to keep. Jesus summed it all up in Matthew 22:37-40 when He said:

> *You shall love the Lord your God with all your heart and with all your soul and with all your mind. This is the great and first commandment. And a second is like it: You shall love your neighbor as yourself. On these two commandments depend all the Law and the Prophets* (ESV).

Your closest neighbor is your husband. So, as you read this commandment from Matthew's Gospel, put it in your heart. Remind yourself daily of Jesus' words. It wasn't a suggestion—it was a command. Is it always easy? No, but it is possible because we have the Holy Spirit of God living in us to empower us to make the right choices in life.

I had just turned nineteen a month before Paul and I were married in 1966. We had met in the Marine Corps while stationed at Parris Island, South Carolina. To say I was a very naïve young woman is an understatement. However, in our ignorance and immaturity, God has brought us through many struggles, heartaches, trials, joys, and celebrations; there were good times and bad times. As we were enjoying an evening on our back porch, Paul turned to me and said, "We've been married fifty-two years. If you could go back and talk to that nineteen-year-old girl, what would you tell her?" I had to think for a moment. Then I said, "I think I would say, 'You're stronger than you think. You're gonna make it.'"

Let me encourage you to keep on keeping on. Keep making the right choices. Keep trusting God. If you are walking in the dark right now, keep walking until you walk back into the light. Jeremiah 29 is such a powerful truth for us to hold in our hearts. He has a great plan for your life.

For I know the thoughts that I think toward you, says the Lord, thoughts of peace and not of evil, to give you a future and a hope. Then you will call upon Me and go and pray to Me, and I will listen to you. And you will seek Me and find Me, when you search for Me with all your heart. I will be found by you, says the Lord, and I will bring you back from your captivity... (Jeremiah 29:11-14).

Seek the Lord! Search for Him with all of your heart. He will hear! No matter what has you held captive, He can and will set you free.

ENDNOTES

1. Steven J. Cole, "Lesson 3: What Do You Mean, 'Submit'? (Ephesians 5:21-24)," *Bible.org;* https://bible.org/seriespage/lesson-3-what-do-you-mean-submit-ephesians-521-24; accessed August 20, 2018.

2. Definition of concubine; https://www.dictionary.com/browse/concubine; accessed August 24, 2018).

3. John Piper, "Six Things Submission Is Not," DesiringGod, February 26, 2016; https://www.desiringgod.org/articles/six-things-submission-is-not; accessed August 25, 2018.

4. Bob Deffinbaugh, "Lesson 15: Taking a Second Look at Submission (1 Peter 2:13-3:7)," Bible.org; https://bible.org/seriespage/15-taking-second-look-submission-1-peter-213-37; accessed August 25, 2018.

5. Jeff Haden, "9 Habits of People Who Build Extraordinary Relationships," Inc.; https://www.inc.com/jeff-haden/9-habits-of-people-who-build-extraordinary-relationships.html;accessed August 26, 2018.

Conclusion

More Thoughts on Submission

Because of all the differing views on the subject of submission, I wanted to give my readers a wide range of thoughts. So, I contacted the leaders of the organization Paul pastors and asked for their help. I knew they could provide a variety of women of all ages, marital status, and length of time married. What a great resource! In addition to my own girls and top leaders in this business, the following women did a great job in sharing their impactful and empowering perspectives on the subject of submission. I pray you will take a few minutes to read each one. (I had to laugh at some of the views and grieve over others because of the heartache some had to walk through. I must admit, I understand them all. I know where they are coming from!)

You may not necessarily agree with all of them, but as my husband always says, "Just eat the meat and spit out the bones." Take what ministers to you and enjoy.

✧✧✧✧

Can I say that initially when my husband and I were married I was thirty-six and back then (almost five years ago) the word "submission" to me was literally as bad as the worst four letter word in the dictionary! I can state that because of my lack of growth and understanding, submission to me meant that I had to go around living my life ruled by a "Macho Male Chauvinist Man." Submission as a wife meant that I had to be under the thumb and rule of a man as I bowed down to him and kissed his feet for bossing me around. So of course I would resist and cringe when he would ask me to allow him to lead or when he would ask me to do something for him. Therefore, we would fight.

How could I, a super accomplished, independent, hard-working woman who had been through enough in life and had fought in a male-dominated world and working field now submit to my husband—who in my eyes was below me because I had accomplished so much on my own. In my mind, *I* was never going to submit, he was just going to have to accept me as the head of the household because I'd broken through barriers of bad relationships and had stood my ground at work and had beat everyone, including men, to be at the top of my field. So, *my* plan was for my husband to submit to me. Amazing how when you have a plan, God hands you His.

Well, here we are almost five years into our marriage. I am now forty years of age, and I can proudly say that the word "submission" means the total opposite of what I originally thought it meant. I've grown so much through this amazing growth journey, not only as a person, but in marriage and in my relationship with God; now, submission is such a beautiful word in my vocabulary. I truly believe it takes a true woman of strength and a strong woman to submit to a man and understand that word as something good rather than something bad. I love knowing that.

Submission to me now means that I have to allow my husband to take me under his wing as he protects me and elevates me to the fullest in life! It's working together as a team and knowing that because our values align, he will fight to defeat anything and everything that gets in our way of the mission we have been handed. To me, submission is allowing him to lead from the front in all aspects of life as I stand by his side. My job is to stand by his side and pick him up when he's down so we can go hand in hand together. If I submit to my husband, I'm letting him know that I trust in his ability as a man and husband to lead his family in the right direction. Because he is a man of God and I trust God, and because he is a mentee to another man who has led others with strength, I know and trust that because he's submitted to God, I will submit to him.

Ultimately, I want my husband to do the same for others, so submission for me means fighting the bad together so we can win over the good. We have to submit to God's will; and I believe that's why God gifted me with someone who could bring me with him by elevating me and protecting me.

—Karla B. Bater, age 40, married 5 years

I always think of the verses in Ephesians 5 about submitting to your husband in everything. I often heard this growing up in church, but I did not actually witness a healthy example of what that looked like. My father was physically and emotionally abusive to my mother, and I watched her "submit" or sometimes refuse to "submit" to him—to protect us children!—and get hurt time and time again. She endured this for too many years before she finally took us and left him. I know she struggled with a lot of guilt and shame because of this.

The issue is, their relationship was missing the other part of the verse—a husband loving his wife as Christ loves the church.

As a married woman, I have struggled to know what exactly submission means. I often picture a drill sergeant and just saying, "Yes, sir!" or "No, sir!" to orders and not being free to offer an opinion or advice. However, it is still my default to take charge and not consider my husband's God-given leadership as a defense mechanism to protect myself.

I know in my heart that is not what God means by submission. I know it's supposed to be a beautiful symbiotic relationship where I am actually trusting in God that He is leading my husband as my husband leads me. I know I am called to be his helper and that does mean offering my thoughts and having a voice—but ultimately trusting that God will lead him to make the best decision for our family.

It is so hard to have the noise of my generation on top of my own upbringing telling me that by submitting that means I am weak and don't respect myself—that I'm being a doormat and don't have free will. I find it extremely hard to defend the concept of "submission."

Even some of my Christian friends raised in church have turned against a more complementarian view of marriage and say that most Christian books on marriage don't apply to their relationship because they don't believe in submission. I think this really means they don't want to submit to God, which I have been guilty of as well.

But there is the other side of the coin. Christian women told my own mother to endure the abuse and keep submitting and she would win her husband over to the Lord. I truly believe that my mom would not be alive today if she had heeded their poor advice.

Submission is a really difficult term for me to understand, and with so many opinions, it's really tough as a young, married woman to know where to find good biblical examples of a husband loving his wife as Christ loves the church, and a woman of strength submitting to her husband and trusting God in the process.

—Chianne Shepherd, age 29, married 9 years

When grace changed my heart, submitting because of obligation or fear changed to submission out of love. My whole world changed and I am freed. It's the surrendering of my wants and will to my husband's authority and completely trusting in his judgments and care. It's never easy and so scary to try, but once experienced with success, it became my joy. I have found it is best served with respect, love, and a sweet kiss.

—Kathy Gallo, age 63, married 44 years

Submission is not an easy task, as we both have different viewpoints on what we believe is right, in our way.

1. I know that God has called my husband to lead our family and is the head of the household, and we as wives must submit to our husband, as unto the Lord (Ephesians 5:22-24). That was an eye-opener for me knowing it is *unto the Lord*.

2. Being a helper to my husband to carry out responsibilities and support him in all his decisions whether I felt it was right or wrong. That's something I am working on getting better.

3. Praying for my husband to have God's wisdom and to be led by God. And also praying for my understanding and strength to do what is right (Jeremiah 33:3; Proverbs 3:5). It's been part of my devotional time to pray for him and my son, too.

4. Respecting my husband with love and unity and with grace and forgiveness (Colossians 3:13-14). My sevenyear-old son reminds me to "not say anything" when I feel I have to argue my point when I feel I'm right.

I strive to be that Proverbs 31 woman and always pray for God's strength and wisdom to guide me to be better every day.

—Rae Ann Hogan, age 46, married 19 years

I am sixty years young. Married for thirty-nine years, three months, seventeen days, and two hours..

When I hear the word "submission" in relation to my husband, I think of feeling protected and safe. It wasn't always that way and I have the bruises and scars to prove it! (Julie doesn't mean Larry physically abused her, she's talking about the struggles they went through.)

—Julie Koning, age 60, married 39 years

I used to think submission meant to be less than the other, unequal. That the one you are submitting to is seen as the master of all decisions and the one submitting was essentially a glorified slave. I thought the person submitting had no voice, no value to add, and nothing to contribute. A lot of my past confusion and distrust toward public figures or stories of people with a faith or religion was partially based on me thinking they must have some sort of low self-image or complex to need someone to be enslaved to them in order to feel important or respected. I've grown a ton since then.Submission is currently one of my favorite words. To be in submission to your husband is literally to be *subject* to the *mission*. To submit does not mean you have no voice, it means that you have faith. It means that you make all decisions together; but when it comes down to it, he has the final say. He was prepared his whole life to be the leader he is today, specifically for you and your family, and this is your opportunity to trust him in that. I believe it would bring a great sense of peace to a marriage to be able to let go of temptation to fight one another and to instead fight for a unified cause. To bite your lip when perhaps you don't see what he sees, and to trust the man God planned for you.

—Kelsey Visscher, age 29, single

Submission is a "four-letter word" in our society today. You can be with a group of women anywhere today, nail or hair salon, someone's backyard gathering, or at your kid's school visiting with the other mothers, and it would seem nothing is off-limits to talk about. Cursing is a casual part of accenting a point, dirty jokes are celebrated as lively conversation. Sexual talk has no limits or lines that you could go "too far." BUT use the word "submission" and their faces contort into a look of shock and horror that you would use such language in a lady's presence.

My husband, Jim, says that submission is a four-letter word to him too! LOVE. It makes him feel loved when I trust him and honor him with my faith in him to lead and make wise decisions for our life together. Certainly, there are times when we discuss a situation or investment and I cannot see what he sees. That is when I submit to walking by faith and not by sight. There are no sulky looks or the withholding of intimacy because I did not get my way. That would be choosing to try to control him and manipulate him to be under my authority. First Samuel 15:23 says choosing to rebel is as the sin of witchcraft and divination. And insubordination is as iniquity and idolatry because you have rejected the Word of the

Lord. That must be why so many men say, "My wife is a witch." Philippians 4:6, *"Be anxious for **nothing**, but in **everything** by prayer and supplication, with thanksgiving, let your request be made known to God."* I would not just be rejecting Jimmy's authority, I would be rejecting the Word of my Lord.

Faith in my Lord is the key to walking in submission. Faith in the One who designed marriage and my identity in Christ. I am the bride of Christ. I am a member of His body. When I read Scripture, I personalize it as though Jesus is talking to me. For example, in my mind, Ephesians 5:22 says, "Judy, be subject to Jimmy as unto Me." So, in reality I am really trusting Christ because He is the head of the church, His body—that's me! To not trust Jimmy is really not trusting God to fulfill all His promises to me. To love me and never leave me, to protect and provide for me as a member of His body and His beloved bride. When I submit to Jimmy, all of God's promises are all still "Yes and Amen" to me personally. Praise God! Trust me, friend, it's your choice. The Lord's design will send you off into the sunset with your knight in shining armor, or you can choose to fly off on your broom alone.

—Judy Head, age 69, married 49 years

The meaning of the word "submission" has dramatically changed for me over the past fourteen years. I'm thirty-six years old and I was married from 2005-2014 (nine years), and for me at that time it meant that I *had* to submit my will, my thoughts, and my opinions to that of my husband. I *had* to trust him to make the decisions for our family, because he was, as the Bible said, the head of my home. I fought hard against this because I couldn't see how God, who designed me to be so intricately strong and passionate, would expect me to lessen myself; and my husband hadn't earned the right for me to be submissive.

Then in 2014, my life got flipped upside down. My husband left me for another woman when I was six months pregnant with our second child. At that moment in my life, submission took on a whole new meaning. I was forced to submit to God and His authority. I could no longer control my life as it felt like it was in a state of constant chaos, and in order to survive, I had to recognize that God alone was in control. So, He wrapped His arms around me as I submitted to Him and His will; and with submitting, His peace and comfort engrossed me. Unbeknownst to me, God was preparing me for the chapter of my life that I am now in.

I am currently dating a man of God and growing in my relationship. At this point in my life, submission no longer means me having to be a lesser version of myself. It means that I *get* to remove my need to control from the equation and completely rely on God for the direction of my life as the rightful Head of my home. It means that I *get* to accept God's authority in my life and that I can fully entrust my mate to Him as he is a steward of God's vision for our lives. It means that I *get* to focus on growing and maturing in my current relationship as we are unified in having God as our Steerer. And the peace that comes from that is so much stronger than the need to fight against it.

—Jyening Rose, age 36, divorced

I grew up watching *Leave It to Beaver* and *Father Knows Best* and many such programs when wives back then were not in the workplace outside of the home. Their hair and makeup were always perfect, home organized, they wore dresses and aprons, and kissed their husbands as they arrived home from work. Dinner was ready and the table was set perfectly. The husband would relax in an easy chair and read the paper as the wife did the dishes and got the children ready for bed. "I Love Lucy" put a different twist on marriage. So funny with a little rebellion and humorous situations.

My parents were divorced when I was three years of age; Jim's parents at age five. Both of us were raised by very strong women who worked several jobs. No role model of submission there. I went to live with my sister who did everything in the house and waited hand and foot on her husband. He was very lazy.

When I married in 1970, I was working to help put my husband through respiratory therapy school. But I always tried to have the house clean, meals ready, and the laundry done, all while working, knowing he would be finished with school soon. As children came along, I continued the routine, but became resentful. I thought of the word "submission" at that time as being a doormat. Even when I attended church seminars on marriage, it was all about serving your husband—not about real communication.

After attending some meetings together, we learned so much about how to understand one another and our proper roles in marriage. Our hearts were softened and we learned about speaking kindly to each other, manners within the home, tone and timing of communication, and truly learning to help one another and to serve each other kindly. This is how I now view submission: treating each other with love and respect and kindness and manners. I now see it is the unselfish way to live. I want to surprise him and do special things for him, and he does the same for me—and we count it all joy.

—Pam Chua, age 67, married 48 years

I have to admit I was tempted to look up definitions and get all theological regarding the word "submission," but I resisted and instead opted for sharing straight from my heart and personal experience. To me submission can be summed up in what my husband and I call "the attitude of marriage." Every day we work hard to help each other become the best versions of ourselves, and every day we put each other's needs above our own. Submission isn't just a woman's role or action, it requires equal participation from both partners. I cannot separate the verse "Wives, submit to your own husbands," without also referencing "Husbands, love your wives, just as Christ loves the church" (see Ephesians 5:22,25).

When these two things happen harmoniously, it is the most beautiful of things!

—Kendra Darwin, age 36, married 14 years

Submission is submitting to a mission. In a marriage, submission is submitting to the mission and leadership that a husband communicates and models to the wife, so that she knows who she is following and to whom she is giving up her freedoms. The mission is a conversation and an agreement that the husband and wife come up with together, but it's what the husband is responsible for when it comes to leading his family. When the husband is a servant leader, he protects and pastors his wife, he initiates and invites the advice and influence of his wife, and she will submit to his ultimate decision making. A wife who submits to her husband trusts that her value and input is considered.

—Esther Zhang, age 34, married 8 years****

At first when I heard this term years ago, I didn't like it. Woman's lib and all. But after studying the Bible and especially Colossians 3:18-21, it is the description of the family. I have a copy of this attached to my lamp on my desk: "Wives, be subordinate to your husbands, as is proper in the Lord. Husbands, love your wives and avoid any bitterness toward them. Children, obey your parents, in everything, for this is pleasing to the Lord. Fathers, do not provoke your children so they may not become discouraged." I believe this is a blueprint, the way we need to be in the family and it is beautiful. If only we would listen! Love is the binding force of it all.

—Fran Kelley, age 64, married 22 years

For me, being in submission to your spouse is a choice willingly made to follow someone and serve them in a Christlike way. Also, as a future wife, the Scripture verse from Ephesians 5:22 speaks, *"Wives, submit to your own husbands."* So instead of trying to be the head of the household, which is my spouse's place, I must be the neck that provides support for the head to move.

—Jordan Chung, age 21, single

When I think or hear the word "submission" in terms of being submissive to your husband, I think of having enough respect for and to him that you are willing to honor his place as the head of the family and the relationship. With that being said though, I believe that being submissive doesn't mean that she, as a woman, gives up her right to share her opinion and input. I believe that it is essential to communicate what your feelings and your thoughts are, so you can work as a team; but at the same time understanding that your husband is the one who is in place to lead the family through his relationship with God.

—Taylor Tsuruda (soon-to-be Mrs. Linck), age 23, single

When I was younger, my definition for submission was very different from what it is today. I grew up watching television shows such as *I Love Lucy* and *The Brady Bunch*. I recall in particular, the Lucy show when Ricky would oftentimes treat Lucy as a child. I can vividly remember several episodes where he placed her across his lap and pretended to spank her as though she were a small child. Fast forward to *The Brady Bunch* and from my perspective, it was an even exchange of leadership in the home. I was raised by both parents and they are still married today. They have been married for fifty-four years.

My parents and culture shaped my belief early on of submission. Initially, I felt that it meant to have a man in charge of my life. I believed that it was easy for me to accept this mindset as the man I married was kind and considerate. To be honest, it was not a subject that we ever brought up in our marriage. I would say we operated more on the Brady Bunch mentality.

As I got older and became more devoted to my spiritual walk, I learned that the definition of submission was to come under the authority or mission of another. It was worded very simply to stay under the umbrella of protection. There was God, the husband, the wife, and the children—if we stepped out of the order and transposed the vertical alignment in any way, we were subject to the storms, rain, and showers of life. Knowing that God does everything in order gave clarity to His will and my position as a mother and wife. Again, please note that this was an easy transition for me even when I didn't know God's will about submission, as my husband is a godly man and it is very easy to follow a man who follows God.

We have two daughters. They are both attorneys and very strong-willed young ladies. I have taught them about submission and the vertical alignment. As attorneys and the cultural we live in today, they questioned submission; but I shared with them my perspective and the blessings of obedience. I also shared with them that just because it's not popular doesn't mean that it's not right. Basically, there are a lot of good things that you can learn from "old school moms."

—Diane Ervin, age 54, married 34 years

When I first heard words like "obey" and "submit," I was a young mother of two and it was coming from my nanny about other kids in her life she was watching—saying they must obey her and submit! I'm a positive person and my real name is Sunshine, but I started brewing up a storm and instantly got cloudy. I quickly told her my children are not dogs and I do not want you talking like that around my kids. Well, I'm sure you can guess that I wasn't a believer at the time.

Since then, what a blessing it has been for me to learn the true meaning of those words "obey" and "submit," learning about the Word, and not standing on my soapbox trying to be the all mighty in charge and take control. It just ended up being too much chaos and unneeded or unwanted stress.

There is a calming and great joy and peace that comes with submission. Our kids choose to obey as I choose to submit to my husband—and wouldn't you know it, none of us turned out to be dogs. Lol!

—Sunshine Fritz, married 11 years

My definition of submission is trusting enough to be obedient even when I may not understand the why.

—Louise Marchant, age 56, married 32 years

When I heard the phrase, "submit to your husband," I thought of taking orders and doing what you're told without question, much like in a parent-child relationship. It made me picture a domineering husband ordering his wife around to do whatever he wanted and her getting treated like a doormat.

That was until I became part of Worldwide and started listening to the leaders share about their marriages and reading the incredible relationship books on the booklist and learned that submission simply means being under the same mission. Now, when I think of that phrase or word, the meaning is completely different. I think of both husband and wife under the headship of Christ and obeying our duties as Christians. Christ as the Head of the household, followed by husband, then followed by wife.

In our marriage for example, my husband and I discuss everything and we both present our viewpoints, opinions, ideas, etc. But I give the responsibility to him to make the final decisions when it comes to pretty much everything. A lot of times I'll ask him if he wants my help in making decisions, which he usually does, and in which case I'll do research if needed, and come up with the best options for him to choose from so he's not overwhelmed with his leadership role in the home.

I understand now that the ultimate authority in my life is Jesus, not my husband. By serving my husband and being in submission to him, I'm obeying my Christian duty as wife, and my willingness to serve, honor, and respect my husband is a direct reflection of my obedience and trust in Christ.

—Jennifer Quimson, age 28, married 5 years

When I think of the word "submission," I envision a husband and wife in a relationship full of healthy communication and respect where all major decisions that affect their family, relationship, and future are openly discussed. Each side is heard and each perspective is respected; but at the end of the day, the husband is the ultimate authority and has the final say in the decision made or action taken for that couple or family. The wife, whether in full agreement or not, chooses to honor her husband's authority as the final say in their household by upholding the decision for their home and family, therefore showing respect to him as the head of the house.

    —Michelle Abbott, age 40, married 20 years

I am 32 years of age and have been married for five years. Here is my definition of submission toward my husband: Once becoming joined together under the union of God, submission is about finding your new roles together. It should not make you lose your identity or take on anyone else's. Submission is allowing my husband to lead but still be a place of comfort and peace when he may lose his way. It is also allowing God to guide him instead of thinking I can change him by myself. Lastly, it is learning to pray for him and with him so that he can be the head and I can be the neck that turns it.

    —Thalia Sewell, age 32, married 5 years

The reason I submit to my husband is because he respects me, listens to me, and *hears* me. I personally do not believe that a person is required to submit to someone who does not respect, listen to, or hear you. That to me is a dictatorship, and I wouldn't submit to that. Submission for me is a two-way street to God and your spouse. When my husband and I discuss something, he always listens to me and then makes the decision that is best for us. For me, if your husband truly submits to God, then it shouldn't be a problem to respect, listen to, and hear his wife's insight. Frank is definitely not threatened by that. It also helps to have you both in our life, helping us to know our boundaries as I learned just in our last visit. This is very easy for me when respect is given. This is just my personal belief and I'm not sure how that aligns with the Word. Perhaps on the fringe because it's pretty clear that a woman should submit to her husband, no buts.

—Lynn Radford, age 58, married 18 years

As a pastor's wife, you might think I have it all together and have been the perfect, submissive wife. Not! I do think thirty-eight years of marriage have taught me a little; however, my earlier days were manipulative, crafty, and I'm sure not pleasing to the Lord! I used the old excuse, do it now, or buy it first, then ask forgiveness later. It usually worked pretty well for me. I am sure that when I did those things, and asked first, the answer would not have suited me.

Yes, I would repent to the Lord and sometimes turn from my wicked ways, but then do it again when the occasion arose. Ephesians 5:22-24 would pop into my head, and tears would flow, and Wade would forgive me for my un-submissiveness. Honestly, if I would submit to God, then I would submit to my husband. James 4:7 says, *"Therefore submit to God, Resist the devil and he will flee from you."*

Most of us also would like to dig up those times when our husbands have not fulfilled all our dreams and promises. He is a normal, flawed person, just like I am. It just takes coming around and admitting that if I submit myself to God, ask the Holy Spirit to take over those things in both of us that need correction, and then sit back and watch Him work, it is an amazing show! Better than anything I could have asked for. Friend, it's best to do it God's way!

—Anne Trimmer, age 71, married 38 years *(Anne is a dear friend. Her husband was our pastor for many years.)*

Very simply, growing up in the church, the general idea of submission to me was very negative. It was kind of like: obey *regardless* if it was right or wrong, *regardless* if you did not feel peaceful about it, *regardless* if it was against what you believe—simply obey whatever authority figure was above you.

Now, after many years and hearing the truth, I believe I have the true meaning of submission in regard to marriage: submission is *allowing* my husband to make final decisions while he regards and respects what I might also be hearing from God; *allowing* my husband to hear from God and me not insisting or persisting to have my thought or opinion fulfilled or put into place; ultimately, being okay with and *allowing* my husband to make mistakes and for it to be a learning experience for both him and me.

In business, submission to me means being coachable, being teachable, receiving wisdom, and most of all applying the wisdom from somebody who has already done what I am trying to do—humbling myself enough to ask for their perspective in their wisdom and then humble enough to apply it.

—Barb Thelen, age 52, married 33 years

At first when I heard about submission to your husband, I actually very much disliked it and simply told him, "We aren't doing that!" I was twenty-five years of age, and we had been married for three and a half years. I simply thought I would lose who I am. I thought submission would mean my husband bossing me around and me having no voice or identity. I thought it meant he yells, "Bring me my slippers and a cold beer!" And, I would have to do that. Now we have been married for eight and a half years and I am thirty-one years of age. I see submission very differently due to great examples.

I believe you can't be in submission to your husband if he doesn't have a mission. For me it means we are working on the same mission for our life together. He is the leader and we work together. I have become truer to me than ever and look up to my husband more than before. It is always a work in progress, but I feel like we work better together now and my voice is heard more than ever.

—Sally Bachman, age 31, married 9 years

Billie, you and I are of the same generation. We heard often in the 1960s the mantra as women that "we could bring home the bacon, fry it up in the pan,

194

and never let him forget he is a man, because we are woman!" What a lie! A lie the enemy fed us through multiple messengers. I believed it as many women did. Despite that, coming out of college in 1974, all I wanted was to be a wife and mother and stay at home raising babies. When that didn't happen—multiple miscarriages and ever-increasing cost of living—I went to work and became a woman to be recognized as a power force with my employer. The more powerful I became professionally, the more my marriage deteriorated for multiple reasons. As my sister puts it, my husband and I could not get past all the pain of the miscarriages and deaths of children. While that is true, I also realize it was because I believed the lie that I could do it all and didn't need a man to take care of me! A ten yearr marriage ended.

Second marriage—twenty-two years, but through that whole time I was continuing to gain power professionally and a voice for issues. My husband became disabled in a car accident and went from being the primary economic source for the family to becoming very dependent. The more I provided the financial resources, the more I emasculated him through the control of the purse strings.

Through both of those marriages I was a woman of faith and believed I was hearing the Lord God's direction for my life. I now realize I was a strong woman, but not a woman of strength. I didn't know how to stop taking charge and admit my own inadequacies or need for another to navigate decisions. I couldn't lean on another because it would be a sign of weakness. I can say honestly that I wouldn't have walked away from that marriage no matter the situation, but after twenty-two years, my husband wanted out. I have now been single for eleven years and here are the lessons I have learned about submitting:

It doesn't make you less of a woman to submit.

Most important, when I keep my mind and heart openly committed to submitting to the "leader," I hear God's voice more clearly and am drawn into deeper intimacy with my Lord God. If I am unwilling to submit to another whom I can see and hear, how can I keep my heart open to submitting to the Lord God's Spirit?

Every woman of strength I know is able to remain soft, vulnerable, and feminine while still being a strong, passionate voice for justice and morality because they have a man who they know has their back, stands between them and the world when needed, or otherwise leads them and their family based on a shared vision of non-negotiable values.

—LaRae Munk, age 68, single

For me, submission is a decision I made many years ago as my faith foundation matured. So, my decision of faith and obedience to submit to the Lord is followed by every day choosing to walk it out in these three ways:

1. Tune In — Listen to the Holy Spirit's still small voice.

2. Turn In — Lean in to the Lord's Presence.

3. Trust In — His perfect provision for my life.

Ultimately, submission in my life is summed up in one phrase: *Thy will Lord,* not my will.

—Vickie Jardine, age 63, married 44 years

I never dreamed this would be such a tough project! I think I finally figured out it's because I feel that a lot of people see me as a "goodie girl" and have my act together! We all know ourselves and we know the good and the bad. Right now, I don't see myself in submission in a major area in my life, so this is a bit exposing if I'm honest about it. Maybe it will help someone.

Tom and I met in college and got married our senior year, which will be forty-seven years by the time your book is out! We are both sixty-seven years of age, have three great sons, two wonderful grandsons, and will soon be including a vivacious ten-year-old girl! We have always felt we have a fabulous marriage in most areas, and I never really thought much about the subject of "submission." We just always worked everything out, mostly by determination and pushing through. There was no back door.

It seems it's been tougher to be in submission as the years have progressed, probably because we know each other so well and know where the cracks are. (You did this before and it didn't work so why should I follow you down another rabbit hole? You're the one who got us here in the first place.)

Opposites attract, and Tom is a super organized thinker and organizer. Me? I'm a "fly by the seat of my pants" type of person. There are certain areas in

life that tick off your spouse, and when you're opposite, you know there's going to be fireworks. We've
learned to not push those buttons! They are usually little things that can irritate you like crazy and
build up in your mind to a mountain. One area is
the "leave on time button." I've learned that I need
to think the time to leave is fifteen minutes before
we're supposed to leave. Does it always work? Nope,
but I'm better—most of the time!

I don't know if this will make sense to anyone, but the
big thing I've been avoiding for a long time is extra
help. It would surprise you to know our "discussions"
in this area. I'm spread too thin with many plates
spinning—who isn't?—and he wants me to leave it
all and go traveling with him. I have all the excuses
in the world why I haven't hired help, most people
would love to do what he's asking of me. The problem for me isn't giving things up, it's getting them
back later. Note: We had a breakthrough in this area
just this week! Hooray! Help is on the way.

People expect perfection—but there are only frustrated perfectionists! There's more give than take;
sometimes I'm good, sometimes I don't do so good.
We don't have all the answers, but know we have a
great life going and we want to impact the lives of
others so we move on, give it to God, and work on
getting better one action at a time.

When people ask how long we've been married,
they're always surprised, so I tell them we found out
the secret! They always want to know what it is. So,
here's what I tell them, "Tom tells me I'm wonderful!" Then I pause and say, "And I believe him!"

—Valarie Gonzer, age 67, married 47 years

To me, submission is a commitment to support my husband in such a way that he may reach his full potential as a man of God. This gives me freedom to become all that I desire and dream of, because I too am submitting to the Lord. This does not mean I am now being a doormat. Submission is something that we all need to understand and embrace.

I love the word "submission." I am now free to be the loving and supportive wife God designed me to be. Submission to me isn't about what a wife or husband can get; rather, that each places their spouses needs above their own needs. Submission is an attitude of living to bless and serve others. Because of all people, Steve is the one I am called first to serve.

It is not about being controlled by him or giving up my voice. It's about loving him and caring for him. It is a privilege to serve Steve. Submission to me just means you're supportive of your husband and the direction he is leading the family. Submission is supporting your mission as a couple and family.

—Ann Wenkler, married 48 years

I was born and raised in Hong Kong and my parent were from China. While we grew up, I saw my mom was always in submission to my dad. My dad was the one who made all the decisions. This was the culture and how I was brought up. The word "submission" to me means security. Now we live in Canada and I am in business with my husband. I know I can express my opinion, but I leave the important decision making to my husband. And I am good with that.

—Jennifer Mak, age 59, married 38 years

Promises You Can Live By

As a young Christian in the late 1970s, I knew I had to start memorizing God's Word, especially His promises. I needed these truths in my life on a daily, moment-by-moment basis. His Word is the greatest weapon we have in our battle against the enemy and "self" who constantly accuse us. The first promise I memorized was Philippians 1:6: *"being confident of this very thing, that He who has begun a good work in you will complete it until the day of Jesus Christ."* This promise has been a constant reminder that God is the One who saved me, He is the One who will keep me, and He will constantly work on me to make me more like Jesus (Romans 8:29).

Years ago, I read a book titled *Don't Waste Your Sorrows* by Paul Billheimer. My friend, God is going to allow all kinds of situations into your life so that you can be conformed and transformed to look more like Jesus. Don't waste these! Trust that God is in charge.

> *Consider what God has done: who can straighten what*
> *he has made crooked? When times are good, be happy;*
> *but when times are bad, consider this: God has made the*

one as well as the other. Therefore, no one can discover anything about their future (Ecclesiastes 7:13-14 NIV).

We really don't know what tomorrow will bring, as it tells us in Ecclesiastes 7. There are ebbs and flows, ups and downs, joys and sorrows, rejoicing and grieving, good times and bad times, and sunshine and rain in this life here on planet Earth. Whether we like it or not, seasons come and seasons go. Sometimes our life seems like the cold, bitter, never-ending winter. Then along comes spring! Oh, I love this season because flowers are blooming, trees are sprouting new blossoms, the weather is warm and wonderful, and everything seems new, like a fresh start.

Summer isn't far behind. Studies show that this season can bring out the worst in us. People feel tired, irritable, and stressed. People get a lot more aggressive and aggravated when the weather is extremely hot. But hold on, the fall season isn't far behind. I love fall. Pumpkins are dotting the fields to provide their luscious fruit for pies and cookies. Fruit is now ready to pick after growing all summer. But, leaves are being pushed off trees to prepare for the winter season.

Yes, it's winter, again. This is how it is in a marriage, and actually in life in general. But God has given us a promise in Deuteronomy 31:8 (Amplified Bible) that we can hold on to in every season of life: *"It is the Lord who goes before you; He will be with you. He will not fail you or abandon you. Do not fear or be dismayed."* Our loving, heavenly Father will not allow more than we can endure. He will make a way of escape so that we can bear it. He will see us through every situation. I love the statement. It didn't come to stay, it came to pass! He will see us through! Hallelujah!

No temptation has overtaken you except such as is common to man; but God is faithful, who will not allow you to be tempted beyond what you are able, but with the temptation will also make the way of escape, that you may be able to bear it (1 Corinthians 10:13).

In Psalm 119, there are 168 verses that talk about the importance of God's Word—precepts, laws, judgments, statutes, testimonies, and commandments. His Word is a lamp to guide us through this life. I encourage you to find some promises you can keep as your own. You will need these truths to comfort, strengthen, and guide you. You will need God's wisdom to face every situation God allows to come into your life. The following Scripture passage is a good one to start with:

Trust in the Lord with all your heart,
And lean not on your own understanding;
In all your ways acknowledge Him,
And He shall direct your paths.
Do not be wise in your own eyes;
Fear the Lord and depart from evil.
It will be health to your flesh,
And strength to your bones .
—Proverbs 3:5-8

About the Author

Billie Kaye grew up in the small South Texas town of Benavides. She had four siblings and a stay-at-home mom. Her dad was an oil field worker. She never realized she was raised poor because of all the Christian love that was in their home.

At the age of eighteen she joined the United States Marine Corps in order to qualify for the Peace Corps. But God had other plans. Billie Kaye Rexroad and Paul Tsika met while both serving in the Marine Corps and married April 28, 1966, in Beaufort, South Carolina.

Billie came to Christ following Paul's conversion in the early 1970s. They have three children who have been married thirty-one, thirty, and twenty-eight years, along with ten grandchildren and two great-grandsons.

Paul and Billie Kaye have been involved together in ministry since 1971 and have authored several books together including *Get Married, Stay Married* and *Parenting with Purpose*.

Billie Kaye has recorded seven Christian albums along with her Christmas Classic released in 2018.

She is truly a woman who perfectly fits Proverbs 31:28: *"Her children rise up and call her blessed; her husband also, and he praises her."*

OTHER BOOKS BY BILLIE KAYE TSIKA

Operation Blessing

OTHER BOOKS BY
BILLIE KAYE TSIKA AND PAUL TSIKA

Get Married, Stay Married

Growing in Favor

Parenting with Purpose

Growing in Grace

The Overcomer's Edge

FOR ADDITIONAL INFORMATION CONTACT:

Paul E. Tsika Ministries Inc

Restoration Ranch

PO Box 136

Midfield, Tx 77458

Office: 361:588-7190

www.plowon.org